JOURNEY WITH GOD

Daily Bible Readings from Exodus

JOURNEY WITH GOD

Daily Bible Readings from Exodus

George M. Philip

Published by Rutherford House

First published 2003
by Rutherford House, 17 Claremont Park,
Edinburgh EH6 7PJ, Scotland

09 08 07 06 05 04 03   7 6 5 4 3 2 1

British Library Cataloguing in Publication Data

A catalogue record for this book is available from
the British Library

ISBN 0-946068-87-9

Typeset by Lynn Quigley, Edinburgh
and Printed by
T.J. International Ltd., Padstow, Cornwall

To my children, John, Ruth and David

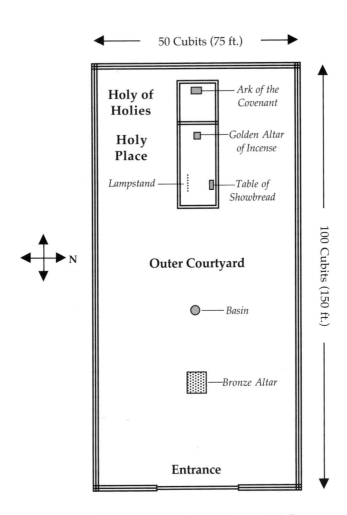

50 Cubits (75 ft.)

Holy of
Holies

Ark of the
Covenant

Holy
Place

Golden Altar
of Incense

Lampstand

Table of
Showbread

N

Outer Courtyard

100 Cubits (150 ft.)

Basin

Bronze Altar

Entrance

THE TENT OF MEETING
(TABERNACLE)

THE BROAD PICTURE

There are many technical questions regarding this book. How did it get its name? Did Moses actually write it along with the other four books attributed to him which make up what is called the Pentateuch, the 'five-volumed' first section of the Old Testament? These matters are best studied with the help of a Bible Dictionary or with a commentary such as that by Alan Cole.[1] That the book and its message are part of the overall revelation of God is clear from Luke 24:27, 44 and from the reference to the 'exodus' (not the 'death' or 'departure') in the story of the Transfiguration (Luke 9:28-31). The message of Exodus is redemption; the setting is history. We read of things that really happened, and God was in them as they developed. The heart of the story is the event of the Exodus, when God delivered his people from their bondage in Egypt and led them to a new land and a new life. This was the event to which the Israelites looked back and of which they were constantly reminded throughout their history (Exod.13:3; Deut.5:6; Josh.24:14-18; Neh.9:7-15). It was when the people forgot that they owed their existence and destiny to God's great deliverance that they fell away spiritually and morally. In the New Testament, believers are exhorted to look back and remember the great deliverance (of which the Exodus was a foreshadowing), when Christ the Passover Lamb was sacrificed for us on the Cross (1 Cor. 5:7; 1 Pet. 1:18-20; cf. John 1:29). The story of Exodus is the story of God's saving activity in the real world of human history. The atmosphere and attitude of the world both then and now is expressed in the words of Pharaoh, 'Who is the Lord...? I do not know the Lord.... I will not let Israel go' (Exod. 5:1-2).

1:1-7

UNSEEN PREPARATION

The opening verses make plain that, although Exodus records a new and significant stage of the work and purpose of God, the events follow on and develop out of the narrative of Genesis, which culminated in the story of Joseph. In Genesis 50:20-26 we have Joseph's testimony to the over-ruling providence of God and the assured statement that in due time God would bring his people out of Egypt and into the land promised to Abraham.

But the beginnings go much further back and if we read Genesis 15:12-16 we see that, mingled with God's purposes of salvation, there are his purposes of judgement upon sin. If we look ahead to Exodus 12:40 we are reminded of how the passing of time is part of God's working. When we pray 'Thy kingdom come', we need to remember also the words we often sing without grasping or being encouraged by their truth: 'But the slow watches of the night not less to God belong'.[2] Why should we be foolish enough to assume that it is only when things are exciting that God is at work? Think of Stephen's great survey of redemption history in Acts 7:9-16, which records how the Israelites ended up in Egypt. Note how Stephen, speaking by the Holy Spirit, brings together the time of the promise drawing near and the emergence of unbelieving, persecuting power set to oppose the people, the work and the purpose of God. Just when the work of God was about to move forward into a new and highly significant stage everything, humanly speaking, began to go wrong. But God had been at work preparing the situation and he was working both to set things in motion and to prepare for the future developments of his plan. The practical lesson for us is that when we start things, we should be clear where they are going to lead, and clear that we are ready to handle the developments.

DANGER IN PROSPERITY

The scene is set by the reference to the increase in the prosperity and influence of the Israelites in the kingdom of Egypt. The whole family of Jacob had arrived in Egypt in order to survive the rigours of famine, but why should that have happened? Was God not able or willing to provide for them in their home territory? We must be careful not to give easy answers to difficult problems but the Genesis stories show how Jacob's family over many years had lapsed from spiritual health and obedience, influenced by the alien cultures around them. It was therefore for their discipline and refinement, as well as for their safety in famine, that they landed in Egypt. Their God was watching over them and guarding them for their future. But the famine days were long past and still the Israelites stayed on in Egypt. It may be that they had no option, forbidden 'exit visas' by Pharaoh's government, possibly because the expertise of these Israelites was a benefit to the economy. The Israelites prospered, and they enjoyed more and more the life and luxury of Egypt. The future story will testify to this (Exod. 16:2-3; Num. 11:4-6). Worldliness, which tends to increase with affluence and comfort, is a creeping disease which debilitates individuals and congregations alike. It distorts people's thoughts of God and leads to compromise and even to apostasy. Read the devastating words in Joshua 24:14. With the passing of time and the easing of circumstances, the people of God began to forget their God and what they owed to him, and what purposes they had been preserved for. Humanly speaking it seems that God's working was being aborted by human perversity. But what seems to be and what actually is are two different things. God is always at work. We need to be careful lest God and his work go on and we are left behind.

1:8-14

NO SIGN OF GOD

Joseph had been the man whose wise administration, inspired by his faith in God, had saved the nation of Egypt in time of crisis. But as the generations passed, his name and influence faded from the political consciousness. As a result, the people who had been of so much benefit to the nation were now regarded as politically and economically dangerous. It seemed necessary to curb the Israelites by legislation lest in time of war or invasion they sided with the enemy. Perhaps the Egyptians feared their nation would be taken over by this growing body of immigrants. A policy of 'ethnic cleansing' was put into operation by means of employment legislation and reduced circumstances. The astonishing thing is that the more they were oppressed the more the Israelites increased. So far there is no mention of God and we must not assume that affliction had turned the hearts of the Israelites to God, although later on the story makes plain that there was indeed a remnant of faith, however weak and hidden. The Egyptians began to have a dread of the Israelites and that led to even harsher attitudes and actions, which made them slave labour. On the one hand there seemed nothing but persecution and increasing hopelessness, but on the other hand there was a people growing in number. There was still a long way to go before the people of God would begin to turn to their God and to cry to him. That does not come until 2:23-25. But God was at work. We sing in worship words which are really full of spiritual encouragement: 'He is least seen when all the powers of ill are most abroad.'[3] F. W. Faber is right when he counsels us to learn what God is like.

> Thrice blest is he to whom is given
> The instinct that can tell
> That God is on the field when He
> Is most invisible.[4]

Why is it that we forget God so easily? It must be a work of the Devil.

BABIES IN DANGER

The ruthlessness of political power is seen here in all its starkness. Economic and ethnic measures having failed to deal with what the Egyptians saw as a threat to their national sovereignty, the new policy of government control of birth and population was put into operation. Some were selected to live and some to die at birth. Government pressure was brought to bear on what we would call the College of Midwives, and no doubt threats of withdrawal of funds would be used to force compliance. It is a terrible picture of political ruthlessness and it has been repeated down the ages to Herod's slaughter of the children when the Saviour was born (Matt. 2:13-18), and on to the horrors of the Nazi regime in Germany when children were used as medical 'guinea pigs'. But we must remember that whenever people begin to interfere with the processes of birth, life, and death, whether by abortion, or genetic engineering, or euthanasia, we move into an area fraught with great danger. Very often such developments are marked by an almost total forgetting of God and the results are incalculable. It is stated clearly that it was because of their faith in God that the midwives stood by their standards of integrity and refused to obey the government edict. They were challenged of course by Pharaoh.

In their answer it is possible that they spoke the truth about the short delivery time of the Hebrew women, and equally possible that they spoke deceitfully in order to escape trouble. It is easy to criticise. Is lying worse than murder? What would we have done? Remember it was a time of barren spirituality with possibly little teaching of God's ways. These women were concerned in principle with the saving and preserving of life, and God blessed them. Pharaoh's only course was to manipulate and enlist public opinion so that the disposing of newborn lives would be accepted as a reasonable thing to do. The contemporary applications are obvious. How much happens now that would not have happened in earlier days, because public opinion, devoid of biblical teaching, is prepared to allow it?

2:1-10

A CHILD IS BORN

The ordinariness of the start of this chapter is quite thrilling when it is set in the context of the significant sweep of God's purposes in history. An ordinary man of faith is married. Some years later, after having two children, his wife becomes pregnant again and a boy is born. These happenings, unimportant and insignificant in the eyes of godless society, were to prove to be events that changed the course of history. Some may have criticised the parents for bringing another child into such a grim and dangerous situation when they already had a daughter Miriam and a son Aaron (Exod. 2:4; 7:7). When we think of the mighty part Moses played in God's purposes we must not forget his parents, whose names very few people even remember (Exod. 6:20), and whose faith in these dark days seemed to make them aware that this newborn child was in some way significant (v.2). In the dangerous situation, in which to defy Pharaoh's edict could lead to punishment and even death, the parents did what they could. There comes a time when the healthy cries of a growing baby cannot be hidden and at that point, in the simple but romantic story of the cradle of rushes, they entrusted the child to God. But faith was neither sentimental nor stupid and the older sister, whose presence by the water would not draw attention, watched to see what would happen. We do not know if Moses' parents knew what their daughter was doing. Miriam was certainly a bright character. Joining the group around the discovered and crying babe, and seeing the tender interest of Pharaoh's daughter, she made the very practical suggestion about a Hebrew nurse to feed him. It was all very simple but God was in it. Did Miriam realise that she was acting as God's significant instrument? We do not always know what God is doing through us, and at times it is best that we do not know. We are so susceptible to pride!

BRINGING UP CHILDREN

The smooth and wonderful working out of the preservation of this child must not cause us to forget the human anxiety that must have been the experience of the parents. Yes, they had faith and had no doubt prayed for the child from the moment it had been conceived. They did not wait for a crisis before they prayed. Many parents wait too long before they pray that their children will be kept for God and led into his perfect will for their lives. Read in Job 1:1-5 how that godly man prayed for his children in the ordinary routine of their lives, and remember the total bafflement that must have shattered him when they were all killed (Job 1:13-22). When Moses' parents put the child on the water they no doubt said, 'He is in God's hands now,' and still they would pray (Heb. 11:23). What did they expect God to do? Were they taken by surprise when their prayers were answered in a way that put their son back into his mother's care for the important early years of training and influence? Remember that Moses was marked out for significant leadership in God's work and for the shepherding of God's people. For that lifetime of work he was taught by his mother, by prayer, precept and example, and there was instilled in him graciously, in a way that did not harm or dominate his personality, an awareness of

God and of God's Word and purposes. This awareness of God stayed with him all his life. His spiritual training in these early formative years was of vital importance in the luxury, privilege and paganism of Pharaoh's palace. But he was also taught and trained in the art of leadership, administration and diplomacy in the secular education he received as Pharaoh's daughter's son. How long Moses' mother was able to stay with him we cannot tell. She may have travelled to and from the palace. That, and the fact that she received wages from Pharaoh's daughter, may have caused other Hebrews to criticise and be jealous. But then, many of those who serve God in evil days are neither recognised, nor appreciated.

2:11-15

THINK BEFORE ACTING

We need the information in Acts 7:22-29 to realise that Moses was now forty years of age. We cannot tell what caused him at that time to have such an interest in the Hebrews, whom he knew to be his people. Nor can we tell what contact he had had with them before this time. What we do know is that, for all of us, times come that are significant. Such a day came for Moses. He had been taught by his mother in his earlier days of the promises of God and that teaching, kindled by the Holy Spirit, made him aware of something of God's purposes for his life. Perhaps in a surge of spiritual awareness he thought that the Hebrews would see him as a hopeful and significant leader in relation to God (Acts 7:25). But Moses was naive. He had lived in comfort, had time to read and study in Pharaoh's court, and had no idea what it meant to suffer the rigour and humiliation of slave labour. No doubt many of the bitter Hebrews regarded Moses as 'one of them', one of the Egyptians. Yes, Moses had a sense of justice when he saw a man being beaten. Taking care that no-one among the taskmasters was looking, he killed the Egyptian and hid the evidence. Had he taken time to think, he would have realised that he had the authority to order the taskmaster to desist and to have him arrested and brought to justice. To take the law into our own hands is always dangerous. The following day, Moses tried to mediate between two Hebrews and found a reaction that was both bitter and resentful. Like many a new minister or missionary, Moses expected too much too soon. He expected an untaught, dejected people to respond in a fully spiritual manner, and that does not happen. Moses was now afraid. The Hebrews knew of his interference and when Pharaoh got to know of it there could be trouble. The only thing to do was to run away. Moses had begun to be aware of his spiritual heritage and destiny. He had been educated to be a lawyer, trained to be a leader, but he still had to learn to be a shepherd and to realise that if you frighten people it is virtually impossible to lead them. A shepherd has to gain the confidence of the flock.

SENT AWAY TO LEARN

I f we remember that Moses was a truly human person then, from our own experience when we have blundered, we will have some idea of how Moses felt when he fled to Midian. We were told in verse 14 that Moses was afraid, no doubt because he saw the implications of what he had done. The New Testament comment on this phase of Moses' life is revealing. In Hebrews 11:24-27 we are told that his departure to Midian was in faith not fear: faith taking control of his natural reactions. Granted he had acted on impulse, but in doing so he knew he had identified himself with the people of Israel and that in consequence he had forfeited all his privileges and possibilities in the secular court of Pharaoh. Knowing the situation with Pharaoh, and having learned so painfully the mixed attitudes and understanding of his own people, Moses realised that the time was not yet ripe for him to take positive action. How things would work out for him, and how the purposes of God for his life and work were to be fulfilled, Moses did not know. The interesting thing is that in the account of his stay in Midian we are told that Moses was content. He did not rebel against his circumstances. He did not sulk with God, feeling that God had dealt harshly with him. Over against the hasty, angry outburst against the Egyptian, which was really a contradiction of his natural meekness of personality (Num. 12:3, AV), we see him showing natural grace and good manners in his dealings with the women who came to water the sheep. Moses' behaviour contrasted so much with that of the other men that there was instantly an open door for him in the home of Reuel (Jethro – cf. Exod. 3:1). Moses was to spend the next phase of his life in the ordinary humdrum obscurity of Midian, working as a shepherd. Perhaps he felt his spiritual service was over. He may have felt he was destined to be a 'nobody' for the rest of his life. No doubt he wondered at times if any of his people in Egypt remembered him. Yes, Moses had blundered, but we should never conclude that a man or woman is 'finished' because of one act, or one phase of life that was defective. Moses was learning and was being prepared. He may at times have felt this, and wondered just what God was doing with his life. He was learning that it is only when we are willing to be nothing that God can make something of us.

IT ALL TAKES TIME

We have been thinking of God preparing Moses for his significant service and we are now told of his getting married and becoming a father. Naturally Moses wondered what God was doing with his life, but there was another significant area that had to be dealt with before Moses could do the work God had planned for him. Today's verses bring into focus the fact that God was working among and preparing the Israelites for the next significant development of their destiny. A prepared leader (and we must not assume too easily that we are ready) is not enough. The people to whom God's leader is to be sent must also be prepared. In Egypt things grew worse and worse for the Israelites. They had been quite happy that Moses had struck the Egyptian guard, striking a blow for justice, especially when none of them could be blamed for the action. But when Moses dared to interfere in one of their own domestic quarrels they resented it. What right had this Moses to tell them what to do? It is a common attitude. Many Christians object to being led by a leader, even when that leader is the instrument of God's blessing to them. How could such a people be a useful instrument for carrying forward into the future the sovereign purposes of God? God left them to live with their situation, leaving them with their discontent, their self-made problems, their shallow spirituality, and with the pressures, pains and manifest injustices of their human work situation. In due time (and it took time, for Moses was forty years in Midian – Acts 7:29-34) the burden was so great that the people groaned. Then, and only then, they began to cry to God. We are told that God heard, God remembered his covenant, God saw and God knew. God had not been indifferent, or ignorant, or forgetful. But real love will wait until it can act for the full benefit and blessing of the loved one. God had been waiting for this cry of prayer, and as he waited he had been preparing his servant. But the answer to the prayer, earnest prayer but not necessarily deeply spiritual, was still to take time to come. God is always ready to act, but are his people and his leaders? God is working at it. Be quite sure of that, and make sure we are all good pupils.

3:1-4

AN ORDINARY DAY?

Even when we study these stories in detail the narrative seems to move on quickly – but we need to remember that for the characters involved years were passing. Moses had been forty years in Midian before he had the experience at the burning bush. Eighty years of his life are now over but we must not think of him as past his prime. He lived for 120 years (Deut. 34:7) and in what now develops we have to recognise that two-thirds of his life were spent in being prepared by God for the mighty work of the final forty years. Ultimately the time-scale of God's working is hidden in the mystery of his perfect will (Acts 1:7). God's working is always long-term and the spiritual ravages of worldliness and backsliding take a very long time to be purged out of the life of even a redeemed, instructed and blessed people (Exod. 16:2-3; Num. 14:1-4; Heb. 3:7-13; Acts 7:35-40). Keep in mind also that God was increasing a people who, in his plan, would take possession of the land of Canaan. Of course, we must not in our day be obsessed with numbers. Sometimes God has to reduce the numbers of his people in order to work safely through them. That is the story of Gideon in Judges 7:2-7. Here in our story a significant moment had come and God broke in upon Moses' life in the course of his ordinary daily work as he shepherded the flock. Whatever the significance of Horeb being called the mountain of God, it is clear Moses had no particular spiritual purpose in going there. His calling as a shepherd had made him observant, and in that climate a bush igniting would not be all that unusual – but a wise shepherd would notice such a thing in the interest of the safety of his sheep. We are told that the angel of the Lord appeared to Moses but at first

Moses was simply interested in a bush that did not burn away. We are not told that Moses had been thinking about God in any particular way nor does he seem to have had any awareness of God at first nor any feeling or 'hunch' that this was going to be a significant day. It was a totally ordinary day. But with God there are no ordinary days. In all things and at all times God is working (Rom. 8:28).

3:5-6

THE BURNING BUSH

The timing was God's timing, and God did a most natural thing that was guaranteed to get Moses' attention. At first Moses had no thought that this 'sign' was significant for him but as he drew near, God spoke to him by name. Moses' reply, 'Here I am', indicated that he realised that in some way *God* was addressing him. This happening, whatever it meant, was personal and important. It would be good for all of us if every time we gather to hear God's Word we give this kind of personal attention. God is always speaking to us in his Word, sometimes with immediate application to our situation and sometimes with truth that should be stored up in mind and heart for the time when it will be needed. Once having recognised that he was in the presence of God and that God had something to say to him, Moses had to be reminded of the holiness of God and the holiness of all that belongs to God. There must be no casual dealings with God. Think of how the young prophet Isaiah, at the start of his ministry, was given a similar sight of the holiness of God. Moses was next reminded that he was in the presence of the active, covenant-keeping, faithful God of Abraham, Isaac and Jacob. That must have brought into focus in Moses' mind and heart the whole sweep of God's plan of redemption ever since the God of glory had appeared to Abraham (Gen. 12:1-3; Acts 7:2). This was the God who began the story and who progressed that story down the generations. He put up with the complications of Jacob, saving the people in Egypt through the ministry of Joseph, that Joseph who gave commandment about what to do with his bones when God led his people to the land of promise (Gen. 50:24-26). This was the God who had preserved Moses at his birth, trained him in Egypt, given him his sense of being part of God's chosen people. This God had preserved and prepared him in the long years of waiting. Moses knew he was in the presence of and in the hand of God who had planned for him, and he was afraid. He was apprehensive. That is not a bad reaction, and certainly better than spiritual presumption.

CALLED BY GOD

What God was about to say and do was not a sudden idea but a plan long settled (Gen. 15:12-16), a plan that Joseph had been persuaded of by faith (Heb. 11:22). Moses was being reminded that he had not arrived at this particular point in life by accident, and certainly not just because of his sins or by the activity of the Devil. We too need to be persuaded of this. All things have been used to serve God's purpose. It is God who has brought us thus far and as his plans begin to come to fruition it is little wonder that we, like Moses, may be apprehensive. In verse 7 Moses was reminded of just how totally and accurately God had been aware of the situation of his people in Egypt. In verse 8 Moses is told of God's plan to deliver them from bondage and to lead them to a land of promise and plenty. Moses is also told that the land is presently in the hands of a host of evil powers who will of necessity have to be faced, conquered and expelled. In verse 10 Moses is told that the action is about to begin. Now all that talk about God going into action was thrilling stuff, but then God made it plain that Moses was to play a significant, active leadership part in the whole scheme of things. That produced a reaction in Moses quite different from his earlier days when he was so sure he was ready to be the champion of the people (2:11-13)! Amongst other things, Moses now had a wife, a family and a substantial career in the sheep business. He protested to God, 'Who am I?' and there may have been a note of mock humility in his voice. God could have replied, 'You are the fellow who got it all wrong in the earlier stages and created complications.' Perhaps it was remembrance of that incident that caused Moses to think God had made a mistake in choosing him. God is never wrong, and he often (but not always) chooses the weakest of people to do his mighty work. When we know our weakness God can use us, because we know the working and the glory are his and his alone (1 Cor. 1:26-31; 2 Cor. 12:7-10).

3:7-12

GOD'S PROMISED PROVISION

In view of Moses' ultimate life of fruitful service, we should give him credit for pondering deeply about the things of God and the promises of God during his years in Midian. He may have prayed many times that God in his mercy would remember his people in Egypt and deliver them. Think how many of us pray with great earnestness that God would work a mighty work of salvation and deliverance in our own land in our own generation. But, do we tend to be like Moses and show real hesitation and reluctance when God is ready to answer our prayers and wants to use *us* in the forefront of his work? Contrary to what we suggested in the previous reading, Moses' reaction may have been one of genuine humility, feeling that he was totally unqualified and far too insignificant in stature to be the leader of such a work. Remember, of course, that some at least of the Israelites had already refused his leadership. God gave his personal promise to Moses that he would be with him, and that signified not only God's personal blessing but also God's power to enable. That is always part of God's commission and it is our great assurance and comfort. We are never sent on God's service in our own strength. Think back to God's wonderful promise to Jacob in Genesis 28:15. Look ahead to God's reassurance to Joshua as he was given the task of succeeding to the leadership of God's people (Josh. 1:2-6). The promise, 'As I was with Moses so I will be with you', should ring in the ears and hearts of all who are called to service, whatever that service is. Think of Jesus' words to his disciples, all of whom were frightened and confused, in John 20:21. *As* the Father sent the Son *so* the Son sends his servants. God confirmed his promise with a sign, but the sign was far in the future and would be seen only when Moses actually went in faith and led the people to serve God at Mount Horeb, which seems to be Mount Sinai. The confirmation of God's presence is the ongoing one of God's blessing on the work and the people.

A GREAT GOD

We need to read this whole passage in order to feel the throb of purpose and the immense detail that run right through it. God was totally clear about his plans, recognising the difficulties that would arise from the people and from Pharaoh, and also exactly how he was going to deal with them. Again and again there is reference to the Person and nature of God, the great I AM, the Lord God of Abraham, Isaac and Jacob. It is as if God was reminding Moses, and us, that he is indeed a great God. This is something we need to recover and maintain in our worship. It is so easy to allow our thoughts of God to become small and narrow to such an extent that, if we feel there are difficulties that to us seem insurmountable, we conclude that God also feels in difficulty. This passage should lift up our eyes to God and should urge us to read such passages as Isaiah 40:18-31; Job 38:1-11; Psalm 19:1; Romans 1:20; 11:33-36. How big is our God? He is great and greatly to be praised (Ps. 96:1-6). But in the presence of God, in conversation with him person-to-person, Moses seemed to be beset with doubts and uncertainties. It was to counter these doubts and fears that God spoke about himself, as if to press in on Moses the certainties, not just the possibilities, for the future with such a God as this. Moses was being constrained to worship, but being more aware of his own limitations than he was of God's almightiness he held back. Read the words of the hymn,

The God of Abraham praise,
Who reigns enthroned above,
Ancient of everlasting days,
And God of love.[5]

AN ENCOURAGING GOD

Moses' doubt and hesitation (v.13) may have had various causes. He may have lost some of his earlier dedication, first manifest in Egypt. He may have been aware of the enormous demand this task would make and felt the 'weakness, fear and trembling' that Paul speaks about in 1 Corinthians 2:3. We could be seeing here the subtle but powerful undermining of a servant of God by the great enemy Satan. We must never forget the Devil. His devices are many and varied and can be manifested in spiritual disguise (2 Cor. 2:11; 11:14). Look back to verse 11 where Moses said, 'Who am I?'. Was this humility or was it doubt and disobedience? 'Self-distrust is good, but only if it leads to trust in God. Otherwise it ends as spiritual paralysis, inability and unwillingness to undertake any course of action.'[6]

God's patient reassurance of Moses is wonderful to see. He was assured that God, infinite, eternal and unchangeable, the God of creation, providence and redemption, the God who is able to do immeasurably more than all we ask or imagine (Eph. 3:20), is the God who has the whole plan perfectly laid and he will be with his servant in every detail of the development. The issues are settled. But note how the great part of this passage has to do with persuading the people of God that God is in fact going to work on their behalf. This was to be the day of God's power, but would his people be ready and willing? There is nothing sentimental about God's word to Moses. There would be difficulties, oppositions, and negotiations over a spell of time. There would be God's acts of judgement and there would be the miracle of finding favour among the Egyptians to such an extent that they would make provision for Israel's journeys. God called on Moses to trust him, and to go forward. Read the passage again and note the recurring emphasis on God. What a God to be involved with in service!

SIGN LANGUAGE

Moses had already been told what to say to the elders of Israel and had been given the assurance that they would listen. Now he contradicts God and says the people would question his spiritual experience and commission. In verses 8-9 God seems to acknowledge that it would take considerable persuasion to make them believe. Moses had not asked for signs but God made allowances for his hesitation by giving examples of divine power, which would impress the hearers of the message. It was God who would give impact to the message, not the signs themselves. Although he is not mentioned we must not forget the presence and the unfettered working of the Holy Spirit. The Spirit simply goes on with his work as the executor of God's purposes. We must not assume signs are necessary or fundamental to authentic ministry and service. John the Baptist, whose ministry moved the whole community, performed no signs (John 10:41) and, in the face of religious unbelief, Jesus refused to give signs (Matt. 12:38-42). On other occasions God insisted on a sign being asked for (Isa. 7:10-14). God is free to act as he chooses and we must not insist that he should conform to what we think is a necessary pattern. If we want to 'interpret' these two signs so that they have a spiritual message, the shepherd's staff could be a symbol of all Moses' natural capacities, gifts and training. These very talents could become a snake to endanger and destroy, but grasped by faith at the command of God they could become a token of God's authority. The staff could be a symbol of Moses' taking up again the work in which he had formerly been a presumptuous failure. The sign of the leprous hand being cleansed could be a sign of forgiveness. Whatever the significance of the signs, God's purpose in giving them is made clear in verse 5. They were to remind the people of their unchanging God of sovereign purpose.

4:10-17

THE CALL REFUSED

Moses had expressed his doubts and fears to God and God had answered with words and signs of assurance. Moses had been shown that he did not need to fear the snake because, in God's power, the 'Serpent' can be overcome (Gen. 3:1, 13-15). Nor did Moses need to fear anything in himself, because all that is meant by sin is overcome in God's redemption. But Moses was still making excuses. His comment on his lack of eloquence was quite irrelevant, because it is God's message that carries the authority, not the human verbal expression of it. Human cleverness and personality can in fact be a disastrous hindrance to the work of the gospel (1 Cor. 1:17). It is godly people God looks for, not gifted people. Again God reassured Moses that he himself would oversee and empower the speaking, hearing and responding to the message. But there was no response of faith or obedience from Moses, and no sense at all of the great privilege that was being granted to him of being a chosen servant of the God of salvation. Compare Paul's reaction to his call from God as expressed in Ephesians 3:8. It is clear from verse 13 that Moses had panicked, and we may see here yet another attempt by Satan to resist and, if possible, frustrate God's purposes. When Moses said to God, 'Send someone else,' God was angry. Why should Moses, or any of us, who owe all that we are, have and hope for to God, be unwilling to serve God when it is made clear that God is calling us? Note very carefully that God took Moses at his word and at that point Moses lost something of the blessing of doing God's will. Aaron was to be the spokesman, the figurehead, and he would be glad to be so. God's people would not have God's first choice to lead them. We must all recognise that if we are unwilling to do God's work, then someone less gifted, less prepared, less capable and less dependable may have to step in and, humanly speaking, God's work might suffer.

THE FIRST STEP

I t is astonishing to see that Moses was not dismissed from his God-appointed work even though at this stage he seemed to be very unpromising material. As the story goes on we will see abundant evidence of the real spiritual stature of this man and this should make us slow to 'write off' people who seem to be persistent blunderers at the outset of their life of service. Think of Peter in the New Testament, who so often got things wrong and yet became a mighty instrument in the hand of God (Matt. 16:13-23). Of course, in the early critical stage of the work, Moses would always be reminded by the presence of Aaron, and by having to speak through Aaron as an 'interpreter', that he had been unwilling and disobedient. But the fact remained that Moses was God's chosen man, and he seemed to be aware of this, because he returned home to Jethro and immediately asked to be released from family duties so that he could go to visit the Israelites in Egypt. He does not seem to have given any explanation to Jethro as to why he wanted to make this move, and there is no mention of his encounter with and commission from God. Jethro's willing concurrence must have reassured Moses, and would have reminded him that God was in this whole situation, opening and confirming the way ahead. God spoke again with further assurances about the main threat to Moses' life being now gone. These reassurances were given, no doubt, to prepare Moses in advance for the resistance and opposition he was going to meet when he confronted Pharaoh. The fact that Moses took his wife and children (and Jethro did not try to dissuade any of them) makes plain that he knew this was going to be a significant turning-point in his life. It was to be a pilgrimage, not a short excursion. Some see a similarity between this story and that of the holy family going by donkey to Egypt (Matt. 2:13, 20). Try to imagine Moses' thoughts and feelings as he started the journey, with the rod of God's authority in his hand. To be trusted with God's work and God's power is both solemn and reassuring.

4:21-23

A HARD HEART

God continued to speak to Moses to make him aware of his presence, and we ourselves need to remember that God is not a distant God, but One who is immediately present with his people whom he sends to do his work. Moses was reminded of the need to be exactly obedient, and he was also reminded that the power that would attend his work was God's power, not his own. Moses was also told to expect opposition of a radical kind because of Pharaoh's hardened heart. But how are we to understand the statement that God would harden Pharaoh's heart, when God was clearly determined to deliver his people? It may be that we are to think of God's intervention in the human situation as being salvation for some but judgement for others – and these two operate together (cf. 2Cor. 2:14-16). In Exodus 8:15 it is stated that Pharaoh hardened his own heart and in 7:13 the simple fact is stated that his heart became hard. No matter what he was faced with, Pharaoh was true to his stubborn, evil heart. The repeated challenge from God to let the people go was the means by which the evil of Pharaoh's heart was exposed. We must not think of God as being perverse and playing a cruel game with Pharaoh saying, 'Let my people go,' and at the same time making it impossible for Pharaoh to do this. The sovereignty of God does not eliminate the reality of moral choice.

'The means by which God hardens a man is not necessarily by any extraordinary intervention on His part; it may be by the ordinary experiences of life, operating through the principles and character of human nature, which are of His appointment.'[7]

We must remember that there can be a succession of refusals of God over many years, none of these refusals seeming to be major or critical, but which build up in time to a total wall of unbelief and disobedience. We need to be careful, lest we are becoming hard of heart in relation to God without being aware of it (Heb. 2:1-3; 3:12-15).

SHAKEN BY GOD

Read the whole passage from verses 18-31 to get the full picture, because only then can we see the significance of the four sections, in each of which there is emphasis on the sure activity of God. God had prepared the situation with Jethro, and Moses may have been deeply surprised by his father-in-law's swift and simple agreement. God then prepared Moses to face, and not to be taken aback by, the inevitable opposition that would come from Pharaoh. Why should we ever be surprised by the dogged opposition of the world? Jesus said it would be so. He was persecuted and we must not expect it to be otherwise with us (John 15:18-21). But what was God now preparing Moses for in today's verses, which begin with the astonishing statement that God met Moses and tried to kill him? If God had called Moses, and opened the way for him to go to Egypt, why did God now stop Moses in his tracks in such a radical way? Most commentators suggest Moses was struck down with a sudden, serious illness, although there may have been a supernatural 'appearance' of God. Some suggest it was Moses' son Gershom who was laid low, because the story goes on to speak of the circumcision of the boy. Now circumcision was the sign of God's 'covenant' and the 'mark' of belonging to God, to God's people, and to God's work. When a father, as head of the family, saw to it that this ritual was carried out, it was a token of the obedience of faith. It seems that Moses had not caused his son to be circumcised. The language of the story suggests that Moses' wife Zipporah had opposed the circumcision of her son, and Moses, perhaps putting the peace of his home before obedience to God, had agreed. There was, therefore, secret non-public compromise and disobedience to God in Moses' life, and that may well have been the source of his hesitation and unwillingness in the encounter at the burning bush. It is clear that Moses now insisted that the circumcision should take place and we must think of this in more detail.

4:24-26

DOMESTIC TENSION

s soon as this 'crisis' came, Moses was fully aware that God was saying something significant to him. As he set out in God's appointed service, Moses knew that this sign of obedience and willing submission had to be performed. The fact that Zipporah seems to have done the operation may suggest she was resentful and would not let Moses touch *her* son, or that Moses may have been too ill to do it. It is difficult, even impossible, for us to understand the meaning of her words but there does seem to be a note of bitterness in them. Her submission to what God required appears to have been in a spirit of anger, perhaps indicating her resentment at God, at Moses and also at her father in agreeing to this whole spiritual adventure. It may have been a shock to Moses, as it has been to many a man of God down the ages, to discover that his wife was not really in sympathy with his commitment to God and God's service (Job 2:9-10). When we read later in Exodus 18:1-7, we learn that Zipporah had returned to her father's home and had no share in the great events of the deliverance of God's people from their land of slavery. But we must see the providence of God in this severing (at least for a time) of the relationship. Whatever the 'shock' administered by God, Moses had recovered and he knew that things were now right between him and his God. He must have recognised sadly and sorely that in the work God had called him to do his wife would have been a hindrance rather than a help. He let his wife and family return home. They were determined to go. Moses knew God was with him and that he would go ahead to do what God had commissioned him to do.

But Moses was human, and we must not forget the sore hurt and disappointment he would have felt. There is a cost in obedience.

BROTHERS IN SERVICE

The fourth element in God's preparation was the arrival of Aaron. While Moses was on his journey and while he was being dealt with by God and being separated from his wife and son, God was speaking to Aaron, who seems to have obeyed without question. Why do we so often forget that God is always active, preparing situations and people and bringing them together at the right time and in the right stage of readiness? These two brothers were different in personality and capacity and yet in the will and work of God they complemented each other. They met at 'the mountain of God', a place that was to figure significantly in the ongoing story (Exod. 3:12), and there they shared God's plans for them. They went to the people, spoke the words God had commanded, and confirmed the word with the signs. God had promised, and the people believed and worshipped. Here again we must see the preparatory work of God's grace by his Holy Spirit. But we must remember that God's preparation of his people for this significant new beginning had been by the sore process of humiliation and suffering over many long years (Exod. 2:23-25). God's people are not always ready to listen, to believe and to obey when God comes to them through his servants and by his Word. Moses had discovered that earlier in his experience (Exod. 2:14). We may point out that this time there were certain miraculous signs confirming that God was in fact speaking. True, but we must also recognise that God had been showing his people the 'signs' of difficulty, persecution, reverses and suffering, over a long period, and these signs had not awakened a spirit of enquiry let alone faith. Often, in the midst of circumstances, we should be asking just what God is saying to us. Human nature always seems to have a craving for signs as if they signified a specially exalted kind of spirituality. But signs are often a concession to weakness of faith and an indication of hesitation in obedience and reluctance to trust. Blessed are those who have not seen (signs) but still believe (John 20:29).

5:1-3

AMBASSADORS

The previous chapter ended with the people evidencing a great spirit of worship, rejoicing and expectation. They were ready to go with God. Perhaps Moses and Aaron, warned and instructed by God, were more realistic in their expectations, and they were proved right. Moses, and Aaron the actual spokesman, went to Pharaoh and with great dignity and God-given authority spoke in the name of God. They acted like true ambassadors, and we must follow their example whenever we speak in God's name in defence or proclamation of the gospel (2 Cor. 5:20).To say the right things in the wrong way simply results in prejudice and resentment and can blind people to the truth. Of course, even when we speak rightly it does not mean that we will get the desired response. Pharaoh gave the classic statement of unbelief in verse 2, speaking with arrogance, contempt and total self-confidence. This Pharaoh regarded himself as head of a mighty world empire with its own great culture, ideologies and religions, and he made it plain that he saw no need for the God of Israel. His words, 'Who is the Lord?', were not a request for information, nor a protest of ignorance, because the Hebrews had been in Egypt long enough for their God to be known. Pharaoh was not denying the existence of the God of Israel but simply refusing to acknowledge him. He was like the people who say that if Christians feel the need to have a God, then it is up to them, but there is no need for others to copy them. In verse 1 it is difficult to decide if the words signify a polite request or a clear demand. The two brothers then spoke in terms of their own faith in God, their dealings with him and their earnest desire to obey him, lest their God should be angry with them. Pharaoh was given the opportunity to change his attitude without any 'loss of face', but he would have none of it. Unbelief can be very stubborn as well as very stupid. If there is any possibility that God is speaking to us, we should pay careful attention.

5:4-9

GOD OR THE ECONOMY

Note that Moses and Aaron spoke of God's festival (v.1) and God's sacrifice (v.3), indicating the God who blesses his people and the God who by sacrifice makes atonement for the sins of his people. Note also that the men spoke of God's people ('Let *my* people go') but Pharaoh regarded them as *his* people, *his* work-force, and he had no intention of parting with them. God's spokesmen addressed Pharaoh on the level of spiritual issues in relation to God, but Pharaoh saw only the political and economic considerations. For him, this was religion interfering with production; religion making the working class rebellious and giving them illusions of power. On the face of it, the request was totally reasonable, involving only three days: a day's journey to the place of sacrifice, a day for the religious exercise, and a day to return. We have to ask if Moses ever intended to return. Was this conversation one of deliberate deceit or just a case of oriental bargaining? We cannot say. In the typical way of totalitarian rulers Pharaoh refused to discuss or negotiate, and went on to use labour laws to stifle this potential stirring of religious feeling and unrest. Religion was equated with political agitation. God had to bow to the state, and the state passed the necessary legislation. Moses and Aaron were accused of being disturbers of the peace, troublemakers (cf. Acts 17:5-9; 19:21-34), and the result was that the conditions of the Israelites became significantly worse, an experience that was not likely to make them more enthusiastic about this 'crusade' Moses was planning to lead them on. Like so many of us in difficult situations and circumstances, when we are told of God's clear plans and gracious purposes, we want to have the immediate answer, without delay or complication. But faith is not learned that way. And, in any case, are we ready for the next stage of God's plan for us?

5:10-21

REACTION TO INJUSTICE

Pharaoh's tactics were both psychological and physical. First he derided the speaking or preaching of Moses, describing the whole business of God's plan of salvation as nothing but lies (v.9). Then the working conditions of the Hebrew slaves were made brutally harsh and every appeal for reasonable discussion was crushed. The cruelty of Pharaoh tells a great deal about the man and his personal and political insecurity. When the slaves protested, Pharaoh said the whole problem lay in their obsessive attitude to their religion (v.17). There is nothing new under the sun. Religion always gets the blame! The leaders of the Hebrew work-force saw how their situation had worsened. They had cried to God (2:23). The answer seemed to have come through Moses (4:29-31) and freedom had seemed so near. They had waited for news of the success of Moses and Aaron in their appeal to the king, but there was nothing but disappointment, so they now cried to Pharaoh (5:15). They did not cry to God. To them, it was clear God had let them down. Everything was worse. Moses and Aaron were waiting for the return of the workers' deputation, whether hoping for good news or waiting to take the blame, we cannot tell. The confrontation in verse 21 was bitter and painful. There was no suggestion that together they should seek the face of God in an attempt to understand and to learn the way forward. There was no hint of faith, just bitter disappointment and recrimination. At this first reverse (and it was a hard one), this first indication that the victory had to be won by faith and obedience, the enthusiasm of the people evaporated. They did not blame God, at least not openly. It was more convenient and more satisfying to blame these God-appointed leaders. That this was a work of the Devil is manifestly clear. God's work was about to move forward significantly, and in such a situation the Devil was bound to try to cause confusion – to hinder, if not to frustrate.

5:22-6:1

WHY?

It was natural for the Devil to attack the man God had chosen and ordained to be the long-term leader, guide and teacher of his people. Moses must have been deeply hurt, but he was also totally perplexed by how things had, in his eyes, gone so terribly wrong. He may well have recalled his earlier attempts at leadership (Exod. 2:11-15), and all his feelings of failure, limitation, insecurity and fear flooded in on him just as they had done at the burning bush (Exod. 4:1, 10, 13). When Moses said, 'Why?' he may have been asking, as faith is allowed to ask, for some enlightenment. On the other hand he may have been blaming God for what seemed and felt a public failure for himself and a miserable and painful reverse for the people. Keeping in mind the further development of the story and the part played by Moses in God's triumph, we must see in Moses a man of real faith, and his faith being assailed by feelings of his own personality weaknesses. We can imagine him saying, 'I'm always a failure. I knew I would not cope. Nothing I do ever works out.' He was wrong, just as Elijah proved to be wrong in 1 Kings 19:1-9. Both these men of God were jumping to conclusions, feeling all was coming to an end when in fact everything was really just starting. This is the significance of Exodus 6:1. God said to Moses, '*Now*, in a way that was neither right nor possible before, things are ready to move.' This does not excuse Pharaoh's evil unbelief and cruel despotism, nor does it excuse the unbelief of the people in their reaction to difficulty. It had revealed the depth of Pharaoh's evil and the rightness of his coming judgement. When the time came there would be no possibility of the Israelites dragging their feet in unbelief or unwillingness, because Pharaoh would in fact drive them out of Egypt. We must learn that God always knows exactly what he is doing with us, and his methods are always right to deal with our personalities, to lead us to faith, and to make us usable beyond our expectations.

I AM THE LORD

Whether Moses turned to God (5:22-23) in faith, perplexity or complaint, or perhaps a mixture of all three, the fact remains that God listened and answered in a most encouraging way. We could regard today's verses as God giving his personal testimony to Moses or we could think of them as the heavenly Commander outlining his clear plan of campaign to his earthly captain. There is no indication that Aaron was present in this interview and, of course, the Israelites were totally unaware of it. They had made plain they thought the whole venture had aborted. The most impressive aspects of this passage are the emphasis on the absolute confidence of God; the clarity of his intentions; and the comprehensiveness of his promises. Go through the passage and count the number of affirmations made by God and the number of promises. It is as if God is saying to Moses that he must remember who *God* is, the greatness of *his* power, and the very real affection and love *he* has for *his* people. Moses had seen so clearly, as he thought, the difficulties and problems of the situation but over against that he had to set the reality of his God. God begins and ends with a clear, unequivocal statement: 'I am the Lord', in every sense of the term (vv.2, 8). If we can grasp this truth we will be able to face many baffling situations with a real calmness because we believe that nothing can ever be outside his control. Power belongs to God alone (Ps. 62:11, AV and RSV) and it is God alone who rules in the kingdoms of men giving power to whoever he chooses and removing that power when it has served its purpose (Dan. 4:17, 25, 32). It is God who works in every situation, causing all things to work together for good in the interest of his people (Rom. 8:28; Phil. 1:12). God reminded Moses that he was the God of the covenant, the God who had committed himself to his people and who would not break his word. Not even the faithlessness of his people will cause God to be unfaithful to them (2 Tim. 2:13). In the great faithfulness of God the future is secure. Such truths about God are wonderfully encouraging and reassuring, but that is only the beginning of what God said to Moses.

6:2-9

THE GOD OF THE COVENANT

Moses was now reminded that God made himself known to the patriarchs of old as 'God Almighty', 'El Shaddai', a name that is often spoken of as 'the all sufficient God'. Moses would have known the Abraham story and may even have had some concept of the call of Abraham in terms of the God of glory appearing to him (Acts 7:2), and his faith and obedience (Rom. 4:3, 18-22; Heb. 11:8-10, 17-19). Abraham believed God, but it was not *blind* faith because God had revealed himself and had spoken his word of promise. Moses was called to believe and to go forward as Abraham did. There is a suggestion that the name 'Lord' emphasises the Person of God and not just his power, and this may hint at the thought of relationship with God and not just service under his direction. This thought is emphasised in verse 7. In verse 5 something of the humanity of God is shown. He has feeling for his people and, no matter what seems to be, he is not indifferent to what they are suffering. God cares. We must never doubt this and never forget it. Our cares and our burdens should always be taken to the Lord in prayer, because he cares for us (Ps. 55:22; 1 Pet. 5:7). Moses was told to return to the people and to tell them these things. Moses' heart seems to have kindled in hope because he went without arguing. The message he was given to deliver to the Israelites was all about God's intentions, which God would carry through by his own power. Count the number of times in verses 6-8 that God says, 'I will'. God was taking full responsibility to redeem, to deliver and to bring his people into the land of promise. It was God, not Moses, who was to bring the people out from under their burden of sin, guilt, shame and bondage and give them new life. And it was all to be very personal as the words 'I... you... my...' in verse 7 make plain. They were God's people by God's choice, not their own. They might have failed in the past and might fail in the future but they could not change the fact that they belonged to God by right of redemption. If we are Christian believers, even when we become prodigals and in stupid rebellion go far from God and waste the substance of our lives, personalities and possibilities, we are still sons and daughters. We are told in the story in Luke 15:11-24 that the Father, because he loves, never stops looking for our return. Then, when we do turn again to the Father, he sees, and while we have still a long way to go, he runs to meet us, to embrace us and to reinstate us. What a God he is! What possibilities are open for our lives because of what he is! We hear the call in Jesus' words to all who are burdened and the promise of rest in the yoke of obedience (Matt. 11:28-30). These truths were spoken by Moses to the people, but they did not listen. We must not be too critical because their spirit was broken and their hopes were crushed because of the cruel cost of life's experiences. God did not abandon them. He knew, understood and cared for them in their need. We must learn to be like God and not to criticise or lay heavy demands on those whose feelings are crushed. Burdens are supposed to be shared (Gal. 6:2).

GOD IS ABLE

Moses had again been disappointed by the unbelief, indifference and unwillingness of his people to whom he had been appointed and sent as God's leader. This is an experience that many ministers and missionaries and others know well, making them react negatively, and be so hurt that bitterness and discouragement become the main influences in life and service. That must be guarded against. Remember how much, how often and how bitterly Jesus was criticised, devalued and opposed, yet he was not deflected from his task. He told his disciples of all generations that they would have the same experiences in the world (John 15:18-21). Moses reported back to God and, although God already knew the facts, it is always the right thing to do to tell God honestly all our feelings and fears. Without pausing to discuss, or reassure Moses about the people, God told him to go to Pharaoh. Moses' reaction was natural. 'If the Israelites won't listen to me you can't expect Pharaoh to listen.' It was a natural reaction, but in the life of faith we are in the realm of the supernatural. Our God is the God who is able. We must never forget his sovereign ability. It is not a struggle for God to cause his will to be done on earth as it is in Heaven, even although it seems to us to be so in the outworking of it. God is able. Read, ponder and thrill to the statements in Daniel 3:17, 18; Ephesians 3:20; 2 Timothy 1:12; Hebrews 2:18; 7:25; Jude 24. Such truths must have been far from Moses' mind because he seems to have been still thinking in terms of Pharaoh being impressed by mere rhetoric. God ignored Moses' words about his limitations, refusing to allow him to dwell on them, and gave him the specific charge to go, there and then, to Pharaoh. Moses went. Never forget that.

6:14-27

BEING PART OF THE STORY

L ists of names tend to be very boring to us but to the Hebrews they were important, firstly because they set the immediate story into the context of the history of the nation and secondly because they identify the main characters on whom God's work now focuses. This family tree goes back only as far as the sons of Jacob, and this may be to signify that the new stage of the work of God in the Exodus of his people from Egypt is to be seen as the final stage in that long historical development which began so much earlier when Jacob took his family down to Egypt in the time of famine (Gen. 46:1-7; 50:22-26). For the Hebrews this reminder would at once make them think further back through the story of Jacob to

Isaac and to Abraham. It is as if this list of names is designed to make God's people of all generations remember that they are not an isolated section of the story but part of the ongoing saga of redemption down through history. We are told here the names of Moses' parents (v.20), without whose faith and courage at the beginning of the story there would have been no Moses (Exod. 2:1-4ff.). The close blood relationship between Moses' parents later became a forbidden area for marriage (Lev. 18:12, 13). When we come to verse 26 and the words, 'It was this same Aaron and Moses', we are being reminded that these men, who were to be seen as giants in the developing story, were real flesh and blood people, the same as the rest of us. Never forget the humanity of those who are called under God to be spiritual leaders. They have human feelings and faults, struggles and temptations, and their usefulness to God often carries with it a depth and extent of cost that few ever recognise. This is seen in its fullest sense in the life and experience of our Lord Jesus Christ, who truly shared our humanity in every way and who suffered, being tempted. Read Hebrews 2:18; 4:15; then read the story of the temptation and never think it was easy for Jesus who, in the fullest sense, was God's Man (Luke 4:1-13).

GOD'S AMBASSADOR

In Exodus 6:26 Aaron, the older brother, was mentioned first (there is no mention of sister Miriam) and the clear commission and authorisation of God are stated. In 6:27, when the picture is of the men standing in the presence of Pharaoh and of the success of the whole venture, Moses stands first. He was God's appointed leader and would be honoured as such in spite of all his hesitation, which earlier had made God angry (4:10-16). In the remaining verses of this whole passage (6:28-7:7), the preparation, call and commission of Moses are completed, and God's servant is ready to go at God's command to do exactly what God has ordered. The narrative seems to take up and develop the discussion recorded earlier in 6:10-12 and brings us to the astonishing statement God now made to Moses: 'I will make you as God to Pharaoh.' A personal ambassador carries the authority and the dignity of the King himself. There was to be a God-given unction upon Moses and, whether or not *he* was aware of it at the time, Pharaoh would know it, and would know that he was dealing not with a mere man but with God. We have an example of this kind of thing in the story of Judges 6:34. The Spirit of the Lord took possession of, or came upon, or clothed himself with Gideon. So it was to be with Moses. The Egyptian court would see and hear a mere man; but in fact they were being confronted by and spoken to by God. Of course, if the human servant of God becomes *self*-conscious about the power attending his service there is instantly the danger of spiritual pride, and the potential for fruitful service is reduced and may even be strangled. Read Paul's words in 1 Corinthians 1:26-31; 3:5-7. Then read 2 Corinthians 4:7; 12:7-10 to see how God's gracious but painful ordering of life enabled his servant to continue to be usable in spiritual service. Moses was increasingly aware that he was dealing with God, and that God was in charge of the whole situation in its every development. Pharaoh was also going to be made aware of God, and it is to that theme the story will proceed.

7:3-7

THE VITAL CHOICE

When we read verse 3 we must not think that in the very process of challenging Pharaoh to let the people go God also made it impossible for Pharaoh to respond. In verse 4 Moses was told that Pharaoh would not listen, and that was no surprise to Moses, who knew the long years of deliberate hardness of heart in Pharaoh and his ruthless oppression of the Israelites. In his great act of salvation and deliverance of his people God would at the same time work in acts of judgement (6:6; 7:4). When the statement is made that God would harden Pharaoh's heart, we must not get confused and lost in the mysteries of predestination, nor must we think of God acting in a sovereign but totally arbitrary way. God said he was going to manifest himself, his Word, and his will to save his people; and he was going to do this in a way that was unmistakable. Pharaoh would know beyond any shadow of doubt that God was speaking, challenging and confronting him, and the effect of the clear presence and personal call of God would be the hardening of Pharaoh's heart. God would go as far as to multiply his signs and wonders, working miracles of power in the presence of Pharaoh as confirmations of the divine message, but the effect would simply be hardening of heart. This is the hardness of deliberate unbelief that will not qualify its attitude nor melt nor change. Unbelief is a frightening thing and its exposure by the power and light of the Word of God leads to hardening unless there is repentance. Right through the Bible, the call to repentance, faith, choice, and response is a real call, full of urgency and tender sweetness. But the call can be resisted and refused, and we must recognise that, in the preaching of the gospel, we are at one and the same time operating as an influence of both death and life (2 Cor. 2:14-16). This is why we must give a clear witness (1 Cor. 14:8) and why we must make sure we listen with the right attitude (Luke 8:16-18; Heb. 4:2, AV), and listen to the right things (Mark 4:24). These emphases have been spoken of earlier in the chapter but they need to be repeated (Phil. 3:1).

7:8-10

A LONG APPRENTICESHIP

At the end of the previous passage we are told that Moses and Aaron set out on their task, and that Moses was eighty years old. In Acts 7:23-29 we are told that he was forty when he fled from Egypt, and in Deuteronomy 34:7 it is recorded that he was one hundred and twenty when he died. Two-thirds of Moses' life were taken up with his preparation under God for the significant long-term work he was called to do. Our generation tends to devalue and to dispense with the need for preparation for spiritual work, and all too often young converts are catapulted into activity for which they have neither the understanding nor the capacity to sustain. Evangelicalism also seems to be preoccupied with short-term work, almost as if Christian service was a temporary phase of enthusiasm and commitment before settling down to an ordinary career. In the story of Moses we begin to see how he has changed from a hesitant argumentative person into a man whom God could trust. We see also how specific God was in his instructions to Moses regarding what he was to do and when he was to do it. This whole venture was not just supervised by God, it was controlled, and that is a message of great comfort and assurance to all who find themselves baffled by developments at any given stage of their work for God. We must never forget that God is a God who prepares both servants and situations and, even when his interventions in the human situation appear to be sudden and miraculous, there have in fact been preparations. We do not in any sense explain away the miraculous element in God's working. God is free at any time to act in whatever way he chooses, by natural developments or by supernatural means. Of course, our trust must always be in God, not in miracles.

7:11-13

COUNTERFEIT SIGNS

As we begin to study the miracles done in the presence of Pharaoh, we must remember that it was God, not Moses or Aaron, who performed them. Note in verse 9 that Pharaoh, so typically of worldly attitudes, would demand a miracle to authenticate the authority of what was spoken to him in the name of God. Our Lord Jesus found the same unbelieving demands addressed to him in his ministry and he refused to grant the kind of signs people wanted (John 4:48; Matt. 16:1-4). Pharaoh was not moved by the miracle of the staff changing into a snake, and promptly summoned his magicians who, apparently without difficulty, performed a similar 'god-like' miracle. But Pharaoh was immediately shown that what was happening was not an equal fight between similar powers because Aaron's staff, presumably still in the form of a snake, swallowed up the others. Be quite clear: in the battle with principalities and powers (Eph. 6:10ff.), there is no doubt as to the issue. It is not a struggle between two equals. Put in the simplest language: Jesus is stronger than Satan. But the other lesson we must learn is that we must not be over-impressed with miracles, because the Devil and his human agents are able to produce signs and wonders that closely resemble the 'real thing'. There is supernatural power that is not of God and we must be very careful not to get involved in a way that can lead us away from God and into the power of Satan. Keep well clear of Tarot Cards, seances, fortune-telling and the like, and be on guard against much of the 'spiritual' language and concepts of the so-called 'New Age' movement. Much that is called new is simply old-fashioned pantheism (God is in everything and everything is God). When told to 'find God in yourself' remember that you find God in Jesus Christ (John 14:8, 9; Heb. 1:1-3). Read and ponder 2 Thessalonians 2:9, which speaks of counterfeit signs and wonders. In 2 Timothy 3:8-9 the two men are traditionally regarded as having been Pharaoh's magicians. In Matthew 7:21-23 it is made plain that some who seem to be committed disciples have in fact no part in Christ's kingdom. We must see to it that we are not deceived by signs and wonders (1 John 4:1).

7:14-25

A SHOCK FROM GOD

This is the account of the first disaster that struck Egypt by the direct intervention of God's power and in consequence of the deliberate hardening of Pharaoh's heart. It is easy to imagine Pharaoh, having been warned, reacting in total unbelief, thinking that this kind of thing could not possibly happen. But it did happen, and we must not try to explain away the miracle of rebuke and judgement simply in natural terms by suggesting that heavy rains had washed down the red clay from Ethiopia making the Nile seem red like blood. Pharaoh would know about such occurrences and would not be likely to attribute the event to God's power. The fact that the change in the water coincided with Aaron stretching out the rod signified that this was not a natural happening. The Nile was regarded as sacred and when it was thus polluted and made foul it must have been a horrendous religious as well as practical experience. The reference to blood throughout all the land seems to refer to the river which flows through the land and possibly to the pools created by the regular overflowing of the river. That the water did not turn into actual blood is suggested by the reference in verse 24 to the digging of wells some distance from the river so that water seeping through the sand would be filtered. This does not explain away the miracle, nor does it require us to regard all floods and their terrible consequences as being judgements of God. But our generation should ask, as Pharaoh refused to ask, what God is saying in the unusual and unexpected things that are happening. Pharaoh summoned his magicians. We are not told how they found water in order to copy and repeat the 'miracle'. All they could do was to add to the disaster. They could not reverse what God had done. They could not turn the 'blood' back to pure drinking water. They had power, but the source of that power was not God. It could only come from another source, and there is no help there for human need.

THE FROGS

In the action of the magicians we have seen Satan's working through the agencies of unbelief, imitating God's power in order to deceive the unwary, and simply making the situation worse. Pharaoh had remained indifferent (Exod. 7:23) and as the week passed he may have dismissed the whole matter from his thinking. But his forgetting of God did not deter God, who once again sent Moses with a message of warning and appeal. Running right through these acts of judgement there is clear emphasis on the long-suffering of God, giving Pharaoh ample opportunity to repent and yield (1 Pet. 3:20; 2 Pet. 3:9, 15). The frog was a sacred symbol in Egypt, not to be harmed, but a plague of frogs, if associated with the flooding of the Nile, would be a huge problem. Those who have heard, in some parts of the world, the noise a small number of frogs can make can imagine what life must have been like for the Egyptians. Read verses 3-4 and shudder. Would the people have dared to petition Pharaoh's Minister of Health to do something? The magicians took action and again added to the disaster, and we must wonder just what their thoughts were. They had power and they believed their own philosophies, but the evil they let loose in society they could do nothing about. That pattern has been repeated in our own day. Men and women started movements in the 1960s which have brought the blight of social and moral decay to the point of disaster in our day, and all they can do now is to blame anyone except themselves. Pharaoh's attitude was that somebody should do something, but nobody could do anything except to make things worse. That is always what happens when God is ignored and when his Word and warnings are refused. The one thing society is doing today is to refuse, out of hand, the idea that a return to faith in the God of the gospel is the answer to society's predicament. How much more in the way of disaster will be needed before a nation and its leaders begin to humble their hearts before God and cry to him for salvation?

8:8-15

A REQUEST FOR PRAYER

Crisis, tragedy, affliction and the loss of social and personal comfort tend to make people pray, at least for a time. We are told that Pharaoh, who had earlier declared that he had no desire to have anything to do with God (Exod. 5:2), now asked Moses to pray for him. He did not ask to be taught about God nor to be taught how to pray himself. This is true to human nature. People are often glad to ask Christians to pray for them and are grateful to be assured of prayer. But what does it signify? In Pharaoh's case it signified simply that he wanted his human situation changed so that he would no longer be uncomfortable and unhappy. Of course, he spoke in plausible language and made promises, just as some people, after a minister takes a funeral service which has touched their hearts because of care and kindness, will say, 'You will see me in church.' They mean it at the time, but it may have little significance. Moses was a wise psychologist when he responded by asking Pharaoh when he wanted this prayer and its answer (v.9). When people ask us to pray for them, perhaps we should enquire just exactly what they want us to ask that God should do. Note that Moses seems to have had no doubt at all that God would answer his prayer, and he said to Pharaoh that he should remember that he was dealing with God, not just with a man. In verse 12 we are shown that already Moses and Aaron were becoming men of faith and prayer. They knew what they had to do. They took the matter to God in prayer and they knew that in this whole developing situation they were servants of God in his work of salvation and judgement. We need to be aware more and more that in prayer, both personal prayer and in the prayer life of the church, we are at the heart of, and are participating in, the power and activity of God. The prayer was answered, but the moment Pharaoh knew relief from the crisis he reverted to his original and obvious unbelief. Without doubt, at every stage his heart was growing harder and harder.

8:16-19

ANOTHER PLAGUE

The third experience of God's rebuke and judgement on Pharaoh came without any warning. The land was struck by an unusually severe plague of gnats, or similar biting insects. More than before, the plague affected the people and animals in their bodies and it needs little effort to imagine the reactions, physical and emotional. If a swarm of midges in our country can chase people indoors, think of what these swarms must have done, especially if hair and clothing were affected. There would be no respite. On this occasion the magicians were shown to be quite powerless and we are to see clearly that, when it pleases God, he allows evil to operate, but when it does not serve his purpose then evil is totally powerless. Those who are believers must not fear evil, even when it seems rampant. God deals with evil in his own way and in his own time. Evil is never free and certainly never has the initiative. We are told that the magicians now told Pharaoh that he and they were being dealt with by God but Pharaoh refused to listen.

His discomfort, his anger and his hurt pride all conspired to make him harden his heart still further. It is suggested that up until now the magicians themselves had not been affected by the plagues but in due time (Exod. 9:11) they too were smitten. Their exposure and their public humiliation became complete. On this occasion there was no sign of Pharaoh being softened at all and this may indicate that his superficial and spurious 'change of heart' recorded in verse 8 had simply served to make him more and more insensitive to God. Circumstances had pressurised him into some kind of 'spiritual' response but clearly it was an emotional reaction, not a genuine turning to God. There is a warning here regarding certain techniques in evangelism which produce a response but which may have the effect of inoculating the person against the real thing! Moses' question back in verse 9 may have been an attempt to test the spiritual validity of Pharaoh's seeming conversion.

8:20-24

A SPECIAL PROVIDENCE

lthough it was not clearly stated earlier, it seems from this passage that up until now the whole land had been afflicted by the plagues. We must consider how the

Hebrews reacted to these uncomfortable experiences. Were they aware that Moses was involved, seemingly as the instigator of all the problems coming on the nation and making their conditions even worse than before? Complaining was to be their normal reaction even after they were delivered from Egypt whenever life became demanding. Right from the time of the Garden of Eden people have always looked for someone to blame, seldom if ever making their first reaction one of asking where *they* have gone wrong and what God is saying to them. If we look back to Exodus 6:6-9 and recognise the spiritual and emotional state of the people, it seems likely that they would not at this stage have been very aware of or responsive to God. The danger of backsliding is that we lose our awareness of God and our sensitivity to him. It is as we live and walk in God's light that we can see clearly and evaluate truly (Ps. 36:9; 1 John 1:5-7). This plague of flies is not to be thought of as simply the result of the decaying bodies of the frogs (Exod. 8:13-14), because there was to be a clear and miraculous distinction between the general territory of the Egyptians and the area of Goshen, where the Hebrews lived and worked. A special providence was to spare and guard the Hebrews, not because they deserved it, but simply because God decided it would be so. On the one hand this was a clear warning to Pharaoh, and on the other, a message to God's chosen people that it was time they became aware of him, his working, and

his plans for their future life, service and destiny.
Pharaoh was left in no doubt that these 'happenings'
were not in any sense accidental or fortuitous. God
Almighty was present, acting and calling for a response
of faith and obedience. When Pharaoh found Moses
and Aaron waiting for him (v.20), he may well have had
a sense of apprehension, and Moses' words made plain
that God was serious. Pharaoh still stood his ground in
unbelief and the very next day the swarms of flies
covered the land. His heart was hardened.

8:25-32

GOD TAKES TIME

Although the narrative seems to suggest that
the plagues followed each other in quick
succession, some commentators, taking
various factors into consideration, suggest
that the whole sequence of plagues covered a period of
at least six months. In that case there would have been
time for the 'news bulletins' about the various meetings
with Pharaoh to spread widely, and we wonder again
what reaction there was in the general population and
among the Hebrews in particular. When the Israelites
became aware that the plague of flies was not touching
them or their territory would they have become aware
of God? As they heard of God's merciful lifting of the

plagues and of his repeated messages to Pharaoh through Moses, would there have been a stirring of spirit at least amongst some of them? We hope so, but we are aware that God can be graciously and solemnly at work in a congregation, a community or a nation, and yet people see only the activity of men and women. At times, when people become aware that God is at work, changing things and constraining them to change their way of life in order to come to a new commitment of obedience, their reaction is to turn away. That is a strange reaction on the part of people who claim to be Christian believers, but it happens. Of course, when there is something wrong in life, people tend to hide from God as Adam and Eve did in Eden (Gen. 3:8). Think of the story of Jacob, who was determined to handle his life in the way he thought best. In Genesis 28:16 he reacted, as if saying, 'God is here and I did not know it.' There are grounds for believing that what he really meant was, 'If I had known God was so near, I would not have stayed here.' Jacob spoke spiritual words but for many years after that he wrestled against God, refusing to learn or to submit or to obey. Pharaoh was the same.

PROUD UNBELIEF

Pharaoh was determined to have it both ways. He wanted peace from God's attentions but he also wanted to have his own will with regard to the Israelites. Like many another godless ruler Pharaoh tried to impose *his* pattern on the spiritual worship and life of the people of God. But when the state controls religion and dictates what believers may or may not do in the area of obedience to God, this must be resisted. Moses was fully aware of this but it is important to note how wise and non-confrontational he was in his approach to Pharaoh. In a sense he appealed to Pharaoh's self-interest. To authorise the Hebrew form of worship and sacrifice would result in riots in Egypt. That would prevent the Hebrews from doing what God had commanded them to do, and Pharaoh would be back in the position of having to be dealt with by God. The three days' journey into the wilderness, spoken of in Exodus 3:18 and 5:3, had to be agreed to, but Pharaoh still seemed to have reservations (v.28). He may have had thoughts about spying on them to make sure they did not go too far. After all, three days' journey into the desert could mean lots of things! Pharaoh added a dash of religion to make Moses sympathetic and he again asked for prayer. Moses was bold enough to warn the king, a risky thing to do with a man like Pharaoh, and then he left the palace. When prayer was answered and the plague was totally removed Pharaoh reverted to his hard-heartedness. Why was he so blind, stupid and stubborn? Had he gone on so long on his chosen way of refusing God that he was now incapable of change? Had the goodness and kindness of God in taking him at his word and delivering him and his people from dread circumstances made him think God was weak and indulgent? Did he not see that the goodness of God was meant to lead him to repentance (Rom. 2:4)? Did the repeated warnings of impending judgement not make Pharaoh think with sober fear? Apparently not. His heart became harder and harder. The more God spoke, the harder Pharaoh became, and in that sense God hardened Pharaoh's heart. This does not mean we should stop preaching judgement and preaching the gospel lest it have adverse effects. It is in the context of and by the instrumentality of preaching that both salvation and judgement are accomplished (Rom. 10:14-17).

9:1-7

TWENTY-FOUR HOURS TO GO

ome see a cause-and-effect link between the various plagues in the sense that the bodies of the rotting frogs and the plague of flies were calculated to spread disease. The plague on the animals may well have been anthrax. If the phrase 'in the fields' is taken literally, we could imagine Pharaoh gathering his beasts into the safety of sheds and stables so that he and his household would be safe, regardless of what happened to the rest of the population. Hard hearts tend to be increasingly selfish when there is pressure and danger. Once again God set a barrier of safety for the cattle of the Hebrews because, in view of their soon-to-be-taken journey to Canaan, the loss of all their beasts would have been a problem in terms of provision for food. But the distinction between God's people and the Egyptians was also a warning to the king. God also made it plain that Pharaoh had not long to think and to come to a decision, because the judgement was set for the next day. How would we react if we thought God's Day of Judgement was only twenty-four hours away? Would we have a great many things in our lives to try to rectify, or would we just not take it seriously? Pharaoh refused to believe what God had said, but the next day when investigation was made among the Egyptians and among the Hebrews, all that God had said had come to pass exactly. Pharaoh must have been aware of a degree of political disquiet in his kingdom because citizens, no matter how ruthlessly they are ruled, do not like to see their whole economic future disappearing. The loss of all the animals meant long-term privation. But still, in spite of all the evidence and all the pleadings and warnings, this man refused to believe. We are told that his heart was hardened. Pharaoh had reached the stage of being judicially hardened by God, confirmed in his own repeated choices and actions

NO PLACE FOR GOD

In our study of the successive plagues and their effect on the population we have concentrated on Pharaoh's reaction, but what about the rest of the people? Were they of like mind to their king? Was the social, economic, moral and political life of the nation so much what they wanted that popular opinion had no desire to change, especially in the direction and pattern of these people of God, whom they had despised for so long? It seems to have been so, for there has been no indication of any unrest among or protest from the people. This is quite understandable if we take time to consider our own nation. That it is in a mess, no-one can deny. There is a rottenness eating at the foundations of society: a moral decay, the consequences of which are becoming evident in all age groups, including children, and in all levels of society. There is a brutality and ferocity becoming more and more blatant and no-one knows what to do. But the one thing most people seem to be clear about is that they have no desire to go the way of godliness, of Christian faith and moral standards. That is regarded as fanatical, puritanical, a contradiction of freedom and personality, and all of it is refused. This is the kind of hardening of heart we are reading about in the Exodus story and it leads to God's judgement. In today's passage even a plague of disease affecting sorely the health of the nation had no effect on either king or people. But God kept on speaking to the king through his chosen messenger, and God kept on speaking loudly to the nation through the stresses of economics and disease. It had no effect. This kind of deafness is an indication that a people have virtually gone beyond redemption. It is all very solemn but we must be thrilled and encouraged by the unquestioning obedience of Moses. Whatever God said to him to say and do he said and did. Perhaps at times as he went to deliver another sermon he wondered if it was worth doing, but he did it. Obedience was his part. The working of power and the planning of methods belonged to God.

EVIL CONFOUNDED

Keep in mind that the magicians, Satan's servants, who had opposed Moses so boldly at the beginning were now not able to stand before him (Exod. 9:11). This is something to be remembered by all who choose to fight against God and his servants (Acts 5:33-39; 19:11-16). Yet again Moses was sent to Pharaoh and the king was left in no doubt that what he was doing was in direct defiance of God. Read verses 14-17 carefully. This man had to realise that there is a God with whom we have to do, a God who sees and tries the secret thoughts and motives of all on the earth (Heb. 4:12, 13). Far from being unduly hard, God had in fact been patient in the extreme with this arrogant king. Pharaoh had been allowed to speak and act as he had done, so that God's name, power and glory might be made manifest in all the earth. That there is a mystery in God's allowing the powers and persons of evil to rise up and work their evil works is undeniable. That Jesus should have chosen Judas as one of the Twelve, knowing from the beginning that he was an instrument of Satan, is also beyond our comprehension (John 6:70, 71). But the fact that God raises up and casts down men and women who do evil does not in any sense remove from these people the responsibility for their actions. God is never the author of evil nor can he ever be tempted to be party to evil (Jas 1:13, 14). Man's sin is his own, and when he chooses to go on in the way of sin, then God gives him over to that kind of life, to its human consequences and to its divine judgement (Rom. 1:18-32). God spoke solemnly and realistically to another king who persisted in evil. His words are in Daniel 5:23, 27.

9:13-26

ALL GOD'S PLAGUES

We have spoken of Pharaoh's hardness of heart in spite of God's pleading and warnings, but still God sought a wise response from this evil man and his people. At last there was some response, as verses 18-21 make plain. It is wonderful and encouraging to be told that, even in the grim, pagan, defiant atmosphere of Egypt, the Word of God was having effect and some were beginning to take God seriously. Perhaps they were motivated mainly by concern for their beasts and their own safety, but at least they were listening to what God was saying and realising that Moses' God was a God who spoke in understandable terms and who meant what he said. The words, 'the full force of my plagues' must have sent a shudder through the population (v.13).

But at the same time some of them believed that this was indeed a God of mercy, willing to spare them even after their long indifference and defiance. The phenomenal storm of hail, thunder, and lightning is described vividly, but we do not need to take literally that each tree and plant was totally destroyed. Of course, in our own generation we have heard of massive hailstones and their destructive power, and of electric storms, wind and floods that have caused astonishing devastation. Throughout history the people of God have suffered in these natural disasters along with others, but in this story, as part of God's testimony that he is the God who saves his people, the people of Israel in Goshen were spared. How they must have stood in awe as events unfolded. As the very creation reeled in God's day of judgement and warning, God himself was their rock and refuge (Ps. 46:1-3). When all manner of crises come upon society, so that it is shaken to its foundations, we tend to say, 'Surely this will make them think and look to God.' But experience testifies that this is not so. Neither will it be so in the final cataclysms of judgement, as is made plain in the solemn and disturbing statements in Revelation 9:20, 21; 16:9, 11. The true nature of God-rejecting people is made plain in that they would rather curse God than believe on him and repent. Pharaoh had virtually reached that stage.

REACTION NOT FAITH

There is no doubt that circumstances and distressing experiences had made Pharaoh afraid, and it would appear that he was at last beginning to be aware that he was dealing with God or that God was dealing with him. His words in verse 27, taken at face value, would suggest that a real work of grace had been done in his heart, but spiritual responses made solely on the grounds of fear and of a desire to escape immediate pressures are suspect. In verse 28 there is a request for prayer and a promise that he would do exactly what God had been commanding right through the story. It would be easy to be taken in by such plausible words and those who have been involved in pastoral counselling know just how careful they must be in dealing with people like Pharaoh, who will promise anything and everything to get what they want. It is not hard-hearted to be realistic, but it is weak to be sentimental. Moses got the right balance, and again we begin to see something of his spiritual wisdom and maturity. He did not hesitate to say that he would pray. That is something we can always do; take it to God in prayer. Moses did not hesitate to express his complete confidence in God. The prayer would be answered in order that Pharaoh and his people might know that the earth is the Lord's. But Moses did not hesitate to say to Pharaoh that his spiritual words of confession and promise were without value because there had been no real change of heart. There was only a desire for relief from crisis, not a heart-willingness to obey God. It was not long before Moses' assessment of the situation was proved right. God was not surprised, and by this stage neither was Moses. God's servant seems to have learned that success in God's work is not easy to calculate, or even recognise. As the story goes on we shall see that prayer also went on. That is important. If disappointment causes us to stop praying, we have given ground to the enemy. Pray on. Pray without ceasing (Rom. 12:12; Eph. 6:18; 1Thess. 5:17).

10:1-6

DON'T FORGET

I t is clear (v.1) that Pharaoh had now moved into the realm of exposure and judgement. God had hardened his heart, confirming this wicked and wilful man in his own often repeated choices. The further plagues and Pharaoh's false dealing with Moses and with God will show beyond any shadow of doubt that he was without excuse (Rom. 1:19-21). The righteousness and the necessity of Pharaoh's judgement were becoming obvious (Ps. 51:4; Rom. 3:4; Luke 23:40-41). The amazing thing has been the long forbearance of God. But in the process evil has been revealed in its full and deliberate nature. The succession of the plagues, both in their coming and in their stopping, has served to demonstrate God's total sovereignty over all the forces of nature. Part of the purpose was that the story of God's mighty acts on the stage of history might be passed down from generation to generation. In verse 2 the phrase in the RSV 'how I have made sport' could suggest that God was perversely playing games with people's lives and that would be a slander on God's character. The NIV reads 'how I dealt harshly' but that again suggests undue severity and that is not God's nature (Lam. 3:32-33; Ps. 103:10). The AV reads, 'What things I have wrought in Egypt.' Of course we could understand this verse in terms of Psalm 2:1-4, where the sure power of God is set over against the puny self-assertive pretensions of men and nations. It is interesting that at this early stage, before the Exodus had taken place, Moses was told to be sure to tell coming generations the wonderful things God had done in the past. God does not change, and what he has done before he is well able to do again. We need to read the stories in Scripture, in church history and in the history of the mission field, to learn what God has done through the instrumentality of his people. Read Psalms 78:1-4; 107:1-3, 8, 15 21, 31; 126:1-3. Are *we* not able to tell of what God has done for us in our own experience? It is a glorious opportunity for witness. It will show people that there is a God who saves.

TIME FOR DECISION

There was a solemn sternness in the warning to Pharaoh, because he and his people knew full well what a plague of locusts could do to the land. Having delivered his message from God, Moses left Pharaoh to think. But Pharaoh did not have much opportunity to think because at that time his servants, perhaps his advisers, made it plain that they thought a change of policy was overdue, and that Pharaoh's insistence on keeping these Hebrews was counter to the good of the nation. When even a totalitarian ruler finds that his 'cabinet' is getting restive, something has to be done and Moses was recalled. But by this time Pharaoh was trapped in his own proud, unreasonable stubbornness and he was determined to negotiate and to get concessions. He still thought and spoke as if he was a man who had real power, even though his pathetic weakness had been demonstrated again and again in the successive plagues. At first, Moses' heart may have leaped with expectation when the words 'Go worship the Lord' were spoken, but immediately there was the qualifying question as to who would go. Pharaoh seemed to be determined that *he* would control the situation. Moses made plain that there were to be no conditions and Pharaoh's answer in verse 10 was contemptuous in tone and content. In verse 11 we can imagine Pharaoh shouting the words, 'No! Go!' The stubborn spirit of this man is almost beyond belief. He could not be reasoned with, not even by his own best secular political advisers. How true are the words of the hymn-writer, 'Blind unbelief is sure to err',[8] no matter what God says or does. That was seen in Jesus' ministry as John 12:37 makes plain. But unbelief traps the unbeliever, as God confirms him in his repeated choices. In this process the unbeliever becomes more and more irrational as well as unreasonable. Note the repetition of 'How long?' (Exod. 10:3, 7), and remember the challenge given by Elijah in 1 Kings18:21. Now is the time to decide to yield to God. Tomorrow may be too late (Isa. 55:6-7).

10:12-20

DECISIONS THAT BIND

orldly people such as Pharaoh tend to refuse to believe that what God says he will do, he will in fact do. Granted there is astonishing long-suffering on God's part, and he is far more patient with rebellious

sinners than we tend to be. But the time of his judgements does come (2 Pet. 3:8-10). We also see in Pharaoh the tendency of worldly-minded people to react emotionally to difficult and dangerous situations. This must never be confused with faith, even if religious and spiritual words are spoken. Pharaoh's bold brashness evaporated very quickly as the swarms of locusts devoured the land. No doubt he was aware of the political reaction of his own people to this economic disaster which they knew could have been avoided. Do you think that Moses and Aaron were in any sense taken in by Pharaoh's apparent 'conversion' in verses 16-17? Do we not all tend to accept too quickly spiritual words and promises spoken under duress? Gripped by fear, and aware of powers operating that he could neither understand nor control, Pharaoh pleaded with Moses, but his words, '*your* God' spoken twice (vv.16, 17), made plain that he did not in any sense yield to God himself. Pharaoh had not changed in any way. In the face of all God's words and works he had hardened his heart. But in doing so deliberately and repeatedly he had slipped into the power of Satan, so that, even though there were moments of panic, he was no longer capable of or even desirous of changing. He had made his choice and God confirmed him in it. His judgement had come. He had been delivered to Satan, and in his case there was no remedy (1 Cor. 5:5; 1 Tim. 1:20). Keep in mind that, in this story of a man reaching the stage when repentance and salvation were no longer possible, a long time had elapsed. The successive plagues took time to operate and in each case there was time for the land to recover. How many national disasters and reverses are necessary before a government begins to listen to God?

DARKNESS OR LIGHT

There is symbolic significance in this plague of darkness, whether it was caused by a colossal sandstorm or by some other supernatural means. It was a darkness that could be 'felt'. There was an ominous element in it, something that the people had never known before. For Egypt it was a withdrawal of light in a total sense, but Israel had light. We are not told how the general population felt at this stage, although in the next chapter we read of various reactions. We are told of Pharaoh's reaction and we see in him the truth expressed in John 3:19. People can choose darkness rather than light. In spite of all that had happened, in spite of all influence and advice, Pharaoh had not moved an inch from his chosen position right at the beginning when he had said, 'Who is the Lord that I should heed his voice? I do not know the Lord and moreover I will not let Israel go'

(Exod. 5:2). Pharaoh still thought of himself as master of the situation and master of his own destiny, but he could not have been more wrong. His first reaction was to seek for compromise (v.24). He tried to bargain with God so that God would adjust his will and purpose to accommodate Pharaoh's unbelief. This is something many people do, trying to persuade God to bless what they have already decided to do. That is not praying for guidance! When told that no compromise was possible, Pharaoh reacted in the way that worldly unbelieving people usually react: he lost his temper. He dismissed the man of God from his presence, told him never to come back, and pronounced his own judgement. Moses confirmed Pharaoh's words in verse 29 but it seems that Pharaoh did not even have a flicker of conscience. Pharaoh, who had been shown again and again to be powerless in the face of God's power, spoke threats to the man who was God's accredited instrument. It may have been that he thought Moses would again negotiate. But he was wrong. There had come the point when God would no longer strive with Pharaoh (Gen. 6:3).

TRUST AND OBEY

Before we go on with the story we must ask ourselves if *we* are in fact listening to what God is saying to *us* in his Word, and in his dealings with us individually, congregationally and nationally. Of course, we can listen, hear and understand and still be unresponsive, just like Pharaoh. He resented God's interference in his life, refused his call, and sought a compromise so that faith and unbelief could be accommodated in his way of life. When told that that was not possible, he rejected God out of hand. The story has concentrated on Pharaoh, but what about the Israelites, who, apart from the plagues of flies and of darkness, must have suffered along with the Egyptians in the disasters that hit the nation. They may well have been very critical of what they regarded as Moses' handling of the situation. They had been critical from the beginning (Exod. 5:20-21; 6:9). They would be critical later, and proved to be critical right through Moses' leadership. When we consider this we begin to see how necessary it was for God to bring the situation to crisis dimensions, because nothing else would have motivated Israel to be willing, when the time came, actually to leave Egypt. We must also consider Moses, who is described now in terms very different from the nervous, argumentative man whose hesitations and excuses at the burning bush had made God angry (Exod. 3:11-12; 4:1,10-14). It seems he had not given way to discouragement, nor had he been deterred by the successive rebuffs from Pharaoh, nor by the criticism of the people. How did he cope with the repeated raising of his hopes as he spoke God's message and then the dashing of these hopes? He knew he was doing God's will, in God's way, according to God's timing. He also knew that God's plan was clear and that the issues were in his hand, and his hand alone. Moses may not have understood the process of God's working, but he knew his labour was not in vain in the Lord (1 Cor. 15:58).

11:1-10

THE FINAL PLAGUE

This last plague was not in any sense to be warning or entreaty. It was judgement, and there was to be no escape. The judgement was to fall in such a way that the worldly Egyptians would see to it that the Israelites got started on their journey without delay and well provided for. In spite of Pharaoh's mad and demonic resistance to every appeal from God it seems that, in the providence of God, the Egyptians had come to have a reverent regard for Moses and for his people the Israelites. It is difficult to understand why the Egyptians should give up their silver and gold. It may have been sympathy for a persecuted people or, more likely, a desire to help the Israelites to go away from their country and leave them in peace. This latter suggestion seems to be borne out by Exodus 12:33-36. We should not fail to note that the very nation that had persecuted the people of God for so long was now, in measure, financing the beginning of their journey to freedom. We are not suggesting that the Egyptians were consciously serving God; we are simply recognising the fact of the sovereignty of God. After all, everything belongs to him by right and he is able to provide for his people in whatever way he chooses. Perhaps we should see here something of God's provision for the eventual building of the Tabernacle, for which precious metals would be required. This does not mean that in our day the church should appeal to secular, unbelieving society for funds for the work of the gospel. What is more, we need to remember that these personal gold adornments proved at one stage to be a terrible snare to the people and work of God, because they were used to make the golden calf of idolatry (Exod. 32:1-6). In today's chapter the final solemn word of judgement was given to Pharaoh, and possibly in a wider more public way (v.8). The death of the first-born had been spoken of to Moses much earlier (Exod. 4:21-23) and, when you think of all that Pharaoh's evil unbelief had brought on the people, you can understand

Moses' anger. That a man should be ready to bring such disaster on his people rather than humble his pride awakened in Moses, the meekest of men (Num. 12:3, AV and RSV), righteous anger, and he is not to be criticised for it. When we see what sin does to others and the suffering it causes, we should be angry.

THE SACRIFICIAL LAMB

Down through the history of Israel as recorded in the Old Testament the people of God were called to remember that it was their God who brought them out of Egypt, the place of bondage; who brought them into the land of promise; and who made them his people to whom he gave his covenant (Deut. 6:20-25; 1 Kgs 8:21). At the heart of the great deliverance and salvation that was the 'Exodus' was the death of the spotless Passover lamb. That this foreshadowed and pointed to the promised Lamb of God is clear in the New Testament in verses such as John 1:29, 35-36; 1 Corinthians 5:7; 1 Peter 1:18-20. Everything about this 'plan of salvation' was specific, detailed and unhurried in its preparation. The Lamb was to be kept separate for four days, then it was to be slain ceremonially, and the blood, signifying that the death had taken place, was to be the mark on the doors of the houses. The lamb was to be the food of the people to sustain them for the journey, and the meal was to be eaten with an attitude of commitment and readiness (v.11). The lamb that was slain according to God's appointment was to be the safety of those people who, believing God's Word, took shelter in their homes marked by that blood. The death of the lamb took the place of the death of the first-born son. For those who by faith trusted themselves to God this was to be the day of new beginnings (v.2). Remember that we are reading history, the account of what God said and did on a particular night 1250 years before Christ was born. But we cannot read the story without our thoughts going forward to the life and death of our Lord Jesus Christ. Even the reference to the roasting of the lamb and the bitter herbs constrain us to think of the suffering of the Son of God for our salvation. The death of the sacrificial lamb was a total action. Everything of the lamb was to be consumed. Nothing more was needed for the salvation of the people. So it was with Jesus, God's appointed Lamb. He died once for all (Heb. 7:27; 9:12, 26, 28).

SAVING FAITH

These verses cause us to think realistically about two solemn and fundamental issues that tend to be forgotten by believers and unbelievers alike. The first is the fact that there is a Day of Judgement. Keeping in mind the long patience and forbearance of God with Pharaoh, the repeated warnings and appeals to repent and to yield to God, and the man's emotional but deliberate refusal of God's Word and grace, we see clearly that the time does come when unbelief comes to judgement. God said the judgement would come, and it did. What happened that fateful night in Egypt is a foreshadowing of the judgement that comes to all: not corrective and disciplinary judgements, but final judgement that separates faith and unbelief for all eternity. Jesus spoke of that judgement and separation in many different ways (Matt. 7:21-23; 25:31-46; Luke 16:19-31; John 8:21, 24) and the apostles also made plain that God had appointed the day when he would judge all men in relation to his Son Jesus Christ (Acts 17:29-31). The second point to note is that God did not then, nor does he now, leave the people without hope. He provided a full and perfect salvation by the way he had ordained, through the death of the Passover Lamb. Of course, the way of salvation having been provided and made perfectly plain by God, the people had to believe what God had said and they had to avail themselves of that salvation. The fact that they marked their homes with the shed blood of the lamb made it plain that they had put their trust in God for their safety in the dread night of judgement. They believed the two facts: the fact of coming judgement and the fact that God, in his sovereign grace, had provided the way of salvation. In Egypt that night there would be among the Egyptians as well as among the Israelites those who believed and those who, in carelessness or self-confidence, refused to believe. So it is to this day when the gospel is preached. God has worked salvation through the atoning death of his Son. The way to safety, to freedom, and to newness of life stands open, but there is a choice to be made. Believe in the Lord Jesus and you will be saved (Acts 16:25-34). None need perish; all may live, for Christ has died (John 3:16-19).

12:14-20

BE IN EARNEST

Without going into too much detail we can recognise this 'feast of unleavened bread' as having been instituted by God as a feast of remembrance to be part of the ongoing life of the people of God, so that they would always be enabled to remember the basis of the salvation that led them into new life as God's covenanted people. The remembrance did not add anything to the work of God in accomplishing the Exodus, nor was it in any sense a repetition of God's saving act. It was a remembering of what God had already done and of the fact that the God of salvation was always among his people to save them. In the same way the Lord's Supper, the Communion Service, is not a sacrifice but a remembering of the salvation accomplished by the death of the Saviour and an assurance that the Saviour is present in the feast, just as he is present in the preaching of the gospel, to be received by faith and to be fed upon as the very bread of life. The feast was to begin on the evening of the fourteenth day of the first month (12:1, 15, 18) and, since seven seems to be regarded in Scripture as the perfect number, there is the emphasis on completeness. There was great stress on the total absence of yeast and, while this points to the fact that, on the night of the Exodus, there was no time to wait for the dough to rise before it was baked, there is a more important emphasis. Yeast ('leaven', AV) seems to be regarded as a symbol of evil being present, and being present it spreads its influence of corruption. Jesus spoke of the yeast of the Pharisees, which is hypocrisy or spiritual falsehood (Matt. 16:5-12; Luke 12:1). Paul, in 1 Corinthians 5:6-13, spoke in solemn and searching terms about the presence of evil in the believer and in the fellowship. This reflected the emphasis here in Exodus on some being excluded from the company of the people of God. We must not misunderstand this. It does not mean that the believer who sins and falls is cast out. There is forgiveness with God (1 John 1:8-9). But anyone who deliberately chooses to refuse God's way of life, even while claiming to trust in God's way of salvation, puts himself in grave danger.

12:21-28

TEACH THE CHILDREN

In Christian worship some people find ritual a help and others find it a distraction or even a hindrance. Whatever the ritual, it is vital that it should be a pointer to God and not something that confuses. All the God-ordained ritual for Israel had great spiritual significance. Hyssop was a common herb and when gathered into a small bunch it was ideal for use, like a rough paint-brush, to mark the door posts with the blood of the Passover lamb. In Psalm 51:7 David prays that God will cleanse him with hyssop and wash him clean from his sins (cf. 1 John 1:7; Isa. 1:18). In the annual remembrance of the Exodus (this account being written by Moses after the event) the people were to stay in their homes the whole night, as if to emphasise that there was no safety in any place other than under the shelter of the death of the sacrificial lamb. On the actual night, as we shall see, the people began their salvation journey during darkness. There may even be symbolism here, for salvation is indeed a movement from darkness into light (Acts 26:18). Note also that in days to come those people who had believed God and had taken his way of salvation were instructed to teach their children the truths of the way of salvation. It is not enough simply to tell children the familiar stories of the Bible and the 'nice' story of Bethlehem. We must tell them why these wonderful things happened. It is not the story of the Cross that constitutes the gospel but the theology or spiritual meaning of the Cross. Right from the time of preparation for the Exodus there had to be concern for future generations, so that in the future the people would not be ignorant of God's way of salvation. It is a rebuke to the church in our day that the population is, by and large, ignorant of the gospel because it has not been truly preached or believed. Note in the last two verses of this passage that the people's worship and their obedience went together. It is obedience that proves faith to be real, and that is where worship begins.

NOW IS THE TIME

Through all the final stages of preparation for the fateful night there had been a note of urgency and this is something we must always remember in the work of the gospel. There is no time for leisurely speculation or consideration, no time to trifle with the urgent issues of the salvation of our souls and the preparation of our lives to stand before God. Now is the accepted time; today is the day of salvation; it is today that God is speaking to us and we have no assurance that we will hear him tomorrow (2 Cor. 6:1-2; Luke 12:13-21). The emphasis on midnight heightens the sense of crisis as we are given the factual account of all that happened. There was alarm in Egypt, even in the house of Pharaoh, whose brash self-confidence was shattered, but his reaction was fear and possibly superstition, a very different reaction from that of the Philippian jailer who was also shaken by God in the middle of the night (Acts 16:25-31). The ordinary Egyptians were also shaken, perhaps indicating that they had been more impressed by God's disciplinary providences than their rulers had been. The Israelites who had believed God were ready and waiting and that is how we should all be living our lives: ready, waiting and well prepared for what God will do. After all, we live our lives in expectation of the promised coming again of our Lord Jesus Christ. Repeatedly in the New Testament we are told to be ready, because in such an hour as we think not the Son of Man will come. Read Jesus' words in Matthew 24:42-44 and Paul's words in Romans 13:11-14 and 1 Thessalonians 5:1-10. Note finally and carefully what is said in the last two verses of the passage. Who would ever have thought that the Egyptians, who for a lifetime had despised and persecuted the Israelites, would deal with them in a way that would provide for their escape into God's future? God's ways are indeed marvellous. He supplies our needs. He does far above all we ask or think (Eph. 3:20; Phil. 4:19).

12:37-42

LIKE A MIGHTY ARMY

The children of Israel, described in verse 41 as 'the Lord's divisions', went out from Egypt like a victorious army. They were aware now that they were a people with a name and a destiny. They knew they were a people with a God who watched over them (v.42). They had been in Egypt for 430 years and, in spite of their slavery, they had increased in number and in flocks and herds (Acts 7:17). The numbers given indicate a vast concourse of people who seem to have gathered from all the areas of Egypt to the place Succoth, ready to be led by God to the land he had promised to give them. It is clear that in the initial stage of this great movement there was a significant awareness of God and, while verse 39 could indicate simply that their food preparation had been hurried, it could also mean, in the light of earlier passages, that the unleavened cakes indicated that they had willingly turned their backs on the dietary luxuries of Egypt (cf. Exod. 16:3; Num. 11:4-6) and that they were now a pilgrim people on a God-ordained diet. Without doubt, at the start of this spiritual 'revival', the people of God began well, with a real degree of enthusiasm and commitment. Such was their awareness of God and their clear commitment to him that they had an evangelistic impact on many of the Egyptians who, seeing a people whose God did wonderful things for them, wanted to follow this God, and joined his people (v.38). We cannot tell if these Egyptians had real faith, or if they were just emotionally attracted, or if they were just tired of living under the cruel, worldly rule of Pharaoh. We cannot tell if the Israelites were glad to have these Egyptians or not. We will think more of this in the next passage, but in terms of witness we should consider Zechariah 8:20-23. Would people want to go with us now because they see that our God is with us?

SAVED TO SERVE

Before considering the 'mixed multitude' (v.38, AV, RSV) who went along with the Israelites, note the fact that no bone of the Passover lamb was to be broken (v.46). Whatever the strict meaning of this regulation may have been, it is referred to with wonderful application in John 19:31-36. All through Scripture the Passover lamb points to the Saviour and his death for the salvation of his people. We are told here that no foreigner or stranger had the *right* to share in the Passover feast of celebration, but at the same time all of them had the opportunity and were invited to become part of the people of God by willingly accepting the 'sign' of the faith of that people, namely circumcision. It was not the *sign* of God's covenant that made them God's people, but the faith that recognised and accepted the salvation and life that God in his grace could give. The Israelites were a chosen people, but they were chosen to be the means of God's blessing to the whole world. That had been made plain right from the start when God spoke to Abraham (Gen. 12:1-3). It was never God's desire to exclude the *outsiders*, and in our Lord's day the bitter and prejudiced exclusivism of the Pharisees stood over against his invitation to all the burdened people to come to him. Some of Jesus' most searching and rebuking words were spoken to those who regarded themselves as God's chosen people. They considered that God's blessing was reserved for them and those they chose to recognise, and barred others from entrance to God's presence (Matt. 23:13-15). In the ministry of the apostles we find the same prejudice on the part of the Jews regarding any suggestion that Gentiles should be welcomed and given entrance through the gospel (Acts 9:15; 22:17-22). God made plain through Moses that there was to be one law, one way of salvation for native and stranger. This we must never forget. Jesus came to seek and to save the lost, not just to bless those already in the fold (Luke 19:10; John 10:7-10, 14-16).

12:43-51

NO ROOM FOR PRIDE

Down the ages of history the gospel has always been preached in a multi-faith, multi-cultural society, and for that reason it is made plain in Scripture that two practical matters have to be kept in mind. God's people are those who have heard his call (in our day responding to the gospel), who have believed in him for salvation, and who have yielded to him as Lord and Master, going after him and learning of him in order to be his servants and witnesses. They have to be a separated people, marked out by belief *and* behaviour as God's chosen people. They are chosen and blessed by him to be his witnesses (1 Pet. 2:9-10), and for that reason they must preserve their separation from the world, not least to preserve the purity and clarity of their witness and message from alien influences. But the preserving of spiritual purity is in order to be a bright shining light that will lead others from all the nations to faith in Christ. That is the great command and commission (Matt. 5:16; 28:18-20). Whoever will may come to Christ and become part of God's people (Rev. 22:17) and when they do come they are to be welcomed, even if they sit in our favourite seat in church, do not dress as we dress, and know nothing of the particular spiritual language which has become a habit to us. If strangers come to our church and we do not greet and befriend them, we are denying the Lord we profess to serve, especially if our neglect is because we are busy enjoying the company of our Christian friends. But God made clear through Moses that the stranger was not allowed to become part of God's people on his own terms. He was not allowed to introduce into the life of the 'church' a pattern of life and activity that would water down and then contradict and conceal God's message of faith and behaviour. The stranger, by submitting to the rite of circumcision, renounced his old way of life, his old identity and inclinations, and became a learner-disciple among and along with the people of God. Of course, we all learn together. There is not one law for the new believer and another for the believer of long standing, except that more is demanded of the believer who has been taught and blessed a long time. We should all ponder these things before we go to church on a Sunday.

THINGS TO REMEMBER

As the story goes on, keep in mind that the great saving deliverance of God's people had been accomplished (Exod. 12:51). They were out of Egypt. They were now a free people, and they were at the first stage of a momentous journey to the Promised Land. The people were reminded that the first-born of man and beast in the whole of Israel were alive and had a future only because the Passover Lamb had died for them and instead of them. There had been a glorious God-ordained and God-given substitution at the heart of their salvation. Because of that, as the people were reminded, they were not their own for they had been bought with a price (1 Cor. 6:19-20). The consecrating or setting apart of the first-born for God was a symbol that the whole of the people belonged to God. They owed their very existence and their identity as a people to God, and therefore they were called to live for him (2 Cor. 5:14-15). We have emphasised again and again that in the death of the Passover Lamb we see foreshadowed the death of the Saviour, and the note of consecration at the beginning of this chapter could be expressed in the words of the hymn about the wondrous Cross, 'Love so amazing, so divine, demands my soul, my life, my all.'[9] Moses then spoke to the people about the importance of remembrance because, as we all know only too well, it is so easy to forget. We must remember that our salvation is the work of God's grace and power and not our own doing. When we were dead in sin, trapped in what we were by nature and hemmed in by circumstances, God acted to save and deliver us (Eph. 2:1-9). But, in further reference to the feast of unleavened bread, the people were reminded that to be God's people means they must put away from their lives all that is sinful. The fact that we have been gloriously saved, that sin's guilt and power have been dealt with, does not mean we are allowed to be careless about how we live. That is a distortion of the gospel and a denial of God's grace (Rom. 6:1-2).

A PILGRIM PEOPLE

The emphasis on salvation, separation from sin and consecration to God does not fully expound this passage. Note carefully verses 4-5 and grasp the emphasis on a pilgrim journey and a future land of blessing and service according to God's promise. We must never lose our sense of future destiny. We are not stationary. This world is not our home (Phil. 3:20). We are on a journey, going places with God. He does not simply set us on our journey, he stays with his people every step of the way and brings us to our destination. It is so easy to settle down to a worldly pattern of life because of the influences around us and the atmosphere in which we live. We need to be reminded of our pilgrim status again and again. Read Hebrews 11:8-10, 13-16, 20-22, 27-28, 39-40; 12:1-2. We live by faith in God's promises (2 Cor. 5:7) and we keep in focus the things that are eternal, even though they may be unseen humanly speaking (2 Cor. 4:16-18). We live our lives standing on the promises of God (v.5). We make it plain that we do so by the way we live and by the fact that prayer and church-going are priorities in their claim on our time. We make it our business in bringing up our children to tell them the meaning and the motivation of our lives (v.8). Without this explanation, our way of life as Christian believers will baffle family, friends and neighbours alike. The Israelites were instructed to make it very plain that they were God's chosen and pilgrim people by certain 'signs' which they wore. These 'frontlets' (13:16, AV) or 'phylacteries' (Matt. 23:5) were pieces of parchment with passages from this chapter and also Deuteronomy 6:4-9 and 13-23 written on them, enclosed in calfskin and fastened to forehead and arms. They were badges of remembrance and testimony, but in Jesus' day the Pharisees had begun to make them bigger and more obvious, drawing attention to what they thought was their spirituality, rather than to God's grace and goodness. Hypocrisy in the realm of God-ordained worship is a great danger.

13:11-16

BELONGING TO GOD

All these regulations about ritual seem strange to us but to the Israelites, at the start and all the way through their salvation journey, they were very important. Again it was emphasised that they had to remember that it was God who in his grace and power had brought them out of Egypt. In the costly dedication of the first-born of the animals they had to remember they belonged to God by right. But did they and do we need these constant reminders? The answer is, 'Yes', because we forget so soon the debt we owe and the vows we have made. The sacrifice of a son was forbidden. He had to be redeemed; that is, another sacrifice had to take the place of the death of the son; another had to pay the price. How we need to be reminded that the Son of God loved us and gave himself for us (Gal. 2:20). When we think of the great salvation with which we have been saved, we need to be reminded that it was God who so loved the world that he gave his only Son (John 3:16); it was God who spared not even his own Son but delivered him up for us all (Rom. 8:32); it was God who laid on him the iniquity of us all, so that we were healed by his sufferings (Isa. 53:5, 6); it was God who made the Sinless One to be sin for us so that we might be justified and accepted (2 Cor. 5:21). We were bought with a great price, and when we think of the company of believers which is the church, our attitude, our involvement and our service must be such that we recognise that it is God's church, redeemed or purchased with blood that was his own (Acts 20:28). But in the life and service of God's ransomed people there is one further thing that must be remembered. In one form or another there will always be the same kind of dogged, deliberate and diabolical opposition such as that shown by Pharaoh (v.15), an opposition that required and received the judgement of God. We must take evil seriously, and that means we must take the Devil seriously.

THE ROAD OF LEARNING

Human nature, being what it is, fallen, complicated and often confused, always wants things to happen quickly. When a sinner comes to Christ or when a believer comes to a real point of consecration, he or she wants a full life of satisfaction and service immediately. No doubt the Israelites, free from Egypt at long last, wanted to be in their promised land without delay. But God had other and wiser thoughts. A people so recently delivered after years of slavery, a people who had already manifested petulance and hesitation, could not suddenly become a well-trained, powerfully motivated army. God did not lead them by the most direct route from Egypt to the land of the Philistines, because that road was well guarded by the Egyptian army and the Israelites would have had to fight their way through. God knew they were not ready for that. No doubt there were the 'hot-heads' (there always are) who were sure they were morally and spiritually ready, and who may have been eager for a confrontation. But God ordained otherwise. He took the people by what seems an unnecessarily long route and there is a deep lesson here. We need to wait upon God and not go blundering forward, even if we are going in the right direction. Jesus made it plain to his disciples that there were things which would yet be part of their experience, but only when they were ready to cope (John 16:12). Think how often Peter created complications by his emotional reaction to situations, in speaking and acting hastily (Matt. 16:21-23; 26:31-35, 69-75; John 18:7-11). In all our Christian service and witness we must give careful consideration to how we say things (1 Pet. 3:15), and to when and in what circumstances we say them (Eph. 4:29). All our lives there is a lot to learn, and some of what we must learn we will consider in our further study of this passage.

13:17-22

LED BY GOD

I f God had led the people by the direct route he could easily have delivered them in battle by miracle, just as he had done in their deliverance from Egypt. But there is more to be learned by the discipline of ordinary experience than by miracle. It is clear from verse 17b that God had spoken to Moses. He made his will known to the man ordained to lead the people, and therefore the journey was to be a directed one. Note further that Moses was very aware of the continuity of the work of God from the past, through the present and into the future. This is the point of the reference to the bones of Joseph, and the instructions he had given so very long ago (Gen. 50:24-26; Heb. 11:22). We need to remember the past, and the debt we owe to past generations, even though in our estimation they were not as spiritual as they should have been. Remember Jesus' words in John 4:35-38. There is a tendency in evangelical circles to ignore, if not to despise, the 'ancient paths' (Jer. 6:16), to forget church history, and to have an obsession with and an almost idolatrous regard for anything and everything that is new and modern. But the faith and obedience of men and women who lived and died for the gospel in past days have much to teach us. How many of us after a long and complicated life with many hazards and afflictions could speak as Joseph did in Genesis 50:19-21? The last two verses of this passage emphasise the great faithfulness and the watchful care of God. Their God went before them and watched over them by day and by night. Recognising their weakness and limitation, God gave them visible and unmistakable tokens of his presence with them. Their God went before them. He knew where he was going. His people had simply to follow in faith.

Guide me, O Thou great Jehovah,
Pilgrim through this barren land;

I am weak, but Thou art mighty;
Hold me with Thy powerful hand....

...

Let the fire and cloudy pillar
Lead me all my journey through:
Strong deliverer,
Be Thou still my strength and shield.[10]

GOD'S STRATEGY

This stage of the story is exciting to read about but it must have been somewhat perplexing and even alarming to live through. It is quite clear that God was giving all the instructions, but the actual directions and place names are difficult for us to determine. The name 'Pi Hahiroth' means the region of salt marshes; Baal Zephon indicates a place of Canaanite pagan worship. The instruction to 'turn back' seems to indicate a significant change of direction, which Pharaoh's spies would report and which would be taken to indicate that the Israelites had failed to find what the Egyptians regarded as the main and obvious route to freedom. Knowing the geography and the exact locations in a way that we do not, Pharaoh would conclude that the host of Israel was trapped by natural barriers, by the Egyptian army behind and by the sea in front. What we have to see is that in verses 1-4 we are being told the story of developments from the standpoint of God's strategy for salvation for Israel and judgement for Pharaoh. Through Moses, the people were told what God was doing but we cannot be sure to what extent they understood. Clearly, the initiative in the whole venture was with God. It always is. God is never on the defensive. In verses 5-9 we are told what was going on in the minds and hearts of the Egyptians. It is remarkable just how soon after a series of significant national disciplines at the hand of God, the Egyptians reverted to a totally materialistic assessment of the situation. They had lost their cheap labour force (v.5) and were determined to redress the situation. There seems to have been no lasting impression left of the solemnity of opposing the God of Israel. They pursued the Hebrews, caught up with them, and no doubt felt totally confident about the outcome. They forgot that it was God with whom they had to do. The enemies of God and of the gospel do forget. That is their folly.

SUDDEN PANIC

These three verses tell how suddenly and totally a wave of unbelief swept over the people of God, this people who had experienced such a glorious salvation, who had been assured of the promises of God and who had been given unmistakable signs of God's presence, both with them and leading them. There is no mention of the people looking for reassurance to the pillar of cloud, which must have been there and visible. Just as the Egyptians had done, so Israel forgot God. Is not this our besetting sin, our first and instinctive reaction when, as far as we can see, things have gone wrong? Without hesitation the people blamed Moses and poured out on him a torrent of scorn, contempt and criticism. We are told that the people cried out to the Lord (v.10), but this does not seem to have been a cry of believing prayer because you cannot pray in faith and at the same time revile the man whom God has set as leader and whose ministry has already carried the signs of God's confirmation. The people jumped to conclusions and said, 'We are as good as dead. It is all your fault. We told you it would not work. We wish we had never listened to you.' The Israelites had cried to the Lord but they had not waited upon him to be assured that what he was doing was right and necessary. Nor did the

Israelites pause to ask from Moses some explanation or encouragement. They jumped to conclusions on the basis of immediate appearances, and when people do that they almost inevitably get it wrong. What the people of God have to do in every difficult situation that seems to have no human solution to it, is to look to God, to cry to him in prayer (which does not necessarily need a long time nor many words) and to grasp more firmly the unchangeable facts of their salvation. God does not do things by half. What he starts, he completes (Phil. 1:6).

14:13-18

FEAR NOT

Note the colossal change that has taken place in Moses. No longer is he the hesitant argumentative person he had been at the Burning Bush, when he was so sure he could never cope with the work God was calling him to do. Faced with strident, unanimous unbelief, already becoming panic, and facing personal abuse and rejection, he never hesitated. He did not reply to the criticism, nor did he defend himself and his ministry. There were far more important things to attend to. There was the honour of God's name, the integrity of the work, and the safety of the people to be guarded. Although it is not stated, are there not good grounds for believing that Moses was aware at once that this was an attack by the Devil rather than just a danger from an earthly power? Moses was a meek man, but not weak, and we see his rock-like character and his wisdom in his handling of the situation. The first thing that had to be subdued was the fear of the people. 'Fear not': because fear is destructive and paralyses. 'Stand firm': which has more to do with 'stop and think' than with 'wait and see'. It was Moses' faith in God and his understanding of God's ways that enabled him to say that they would see God working his salvation. It was God who had led them thus far and who had promised to lead them to the land he had planned. Humanly speaking it seemed to be deadlock, but God is not limited in the way we are. It is what we know of God that must be our rock, refuge and assurance (Ps. 46:1-3, 6-7, 10-11). The people may well have asked why God was dealing with them in this most alarming way. The answer was that God was wanting to show them his total sufficiency and trustworthiness so that their faith would be encouraged and strengthened for the future. The Devil was seeking to destroy their faith, to steal their peace; but Moses was saying, 'If God is for us, who can be against us?' (Rom. 8:31). There are many times when the most spiritual thing we can do is to stop our rushing around because we are simply causing sand-storms that conceal God from the eyes of faith.

GO FORWARD

Moses had scarcely finished his message of assurance, telling the people that the issues were safe in the hand of God and that there would be no delay in his action, when God seemed to contradict what Moses had said. Moses had said to stand still and God almost immediately said they had to go forward. Was there a contradiction? No! Having stood still and quietened their panic, they could hear clearly what God was saying. They were being commanded to go forward in faith. Nothing but faith was of any use, because the way ahead, as far as they could see, was barred by the vast waters the Red Sea. There was absolutely nothing they could do but put their trust in God. We need to be instructed in faith by the study of the Scriptures so that, learning what God is like, we know him well enough to trust him. But we also need to be instructed by circumstances, and this is the kind of thing Paul spoke about in 2 Corinthians 1:8-10. We have commented on how God had forged a new spiritual confidence in Moses, but that is not the same as self-confidence, and it is all too easy to lapse into an attitude in which we go to God's service in our own strength. We must look to God and do what he says, even if the way to do it seems beyond us to the point of impossibility. In Philippians

3:3 Paul speaks of having no confidence in the flesh, but that is not a denial of nor an ignoring of our God-given capacities, talents and gifts. All God has given us must be used in the work God has prepared us for. But it is God who does the work, creates the openings, and adds the increase (1 Cor. 3:5-7). Did the people hear God's words to Moses in verses 15-18? Certainly it was by faith that they crossed the sea (Heb. 11:29); faith in God and trust in their leader. Their experience of fear and bafflement would stand them in good stead in the future. When we are perplexed by God's dealings with us it is good to read Job 23:1-10.

GOD WITH US

I t takes real faith to believe when God commands something as radical as dividing the sea. A great responsibility rested on Moses, who did not hesitate. What we have to see is that the God who challenged the people to have faith instantly gave great and wonderful reassurance and encouragement. The whole point about the pillar of cloud is that God himself was in it. It was God who moved to be the defence of the people throughout the night so that they could sleep in peace. One immediate result was, of course, that the threatening Egyptian army was out of sight. That would have in measure allayed the fears of the people. They would also be able to think that their safety came from the Lord who in Person stood between them and the enemy. Read Psalm 121 and think not only of our safety but of our going out and coming in being kept by God. Read Psalm 23 and think of God with us in the darkest of valleys and of God spreading a table of blessing for us in the very presence of the enemy. It is a truly wonderful thought to be reminded of God being round about his people (Ps. 125:2), and it is a great corrective to fear to be reminded that the very hosts of God, unseen as they usually are, are round us in defence (2 Kgs 6:15-17). The picture of the cloud standing guard over the people as they anticipated the great challenge and adventure before them reminds us of the peace of God that stands guard over our minds and hearts (Phil. 4:4-7). There are so many exhortations right through Scripture saying, 'Fear not!' After all, our times and all their changes and developments really are in God's good, safe, sure, strong and gentle hands (Ps. 31:14-16). The cloud was darkness to the Egyptians and light to the Israelites (v.20). God was giving gentle reassuring light to his people. Crisis never seems so frightening when it is light. The Egyptians may have remembered the darkness of one of the plagues and been apprehensive. Through the darkness God certainly kept an eye on the enemy. He does watch, and he misses nothing.

THE GOD OF CREATION

We cannot explain, and certainly do not want to explain away, the dividing of the waters. It was a miracle. It was God's doing. The stretching out of Moses' hand, holding the staff of God's authority which he had carried in Egypt (Exod. 7:9), signified that God was acting for his people's salvation. The strong east wind, which caused the amazing ebbing of the waters, was the direct action of God the Creator. This was not a natural ebb-tide. The waters were under divine control and formed a walled passage, firstly to allow the Israelites to cross directly and secondly to prevent Pharaoh's armies from trying to overtake on either side and so trap God's people. The difficulty some have in accepting this miracle of deliverance, which seems to involve the disturbance of the natural laws of nature, stems from a limited idea of God. We are told in the creation story that God separated the waters in his sovereign power (Gen. 1:7). In the New Testament we are told that Jesus controlled the wind and the waves, so that even his disciples marvelled (Mark 4:35-41). In the story of Jonah we are told that God controlled the storm, the great fish, and even the booking of berths on a ship (Jonah 1:3-4, 17). How the ground became firm enough to allow the huge company of Israelites to cross, we cannot explain, nor can we explain how so quickly the ground again became soft enough to clog the chariot wheels. What we must see, and see very clearly, is God's action, intervening to save his people. We must learn to let God be God and we must recognise that he is sovereignly free to act when and in whatever manner he pleases. The Egyptians, urged on by their demonic leader, were brash enough to assume that what Israel could do they could do, and they barged into the middle of the sea. Again God acted (v.24) and there is a vivid picture of this given in Psalm 77:16-20. Suddenly, but too late, the Egyptians realised yet again that there was indeed a God with whom they had to deal.

14: 21 - 31

DEFIANCE JUDGED

No-one should find it easy to read about God's judgements. But the reality of judgement, both in history and in the world to come, is spoken of right through Scripture. Our difficulty in grasping the necessity and the righteous nature of judgement lies in the fact that we tend to have a shallow understanding of evil and of what evil does to people and to the work of God. We tend not to think of the offence that evil is to God, nor of his totally righteous and balanced attitude to it. The great New Testament exposition of the gospel as the power of God unto salvation begins with the statement that the wrath of God is revealed against all ungodliness, from which flows all unrighteousness (Rom. 1:18-20). But the Bible also makes plain that God finds no pleasure in the death of the wicked (Ezek. 18:23, 32; 33:11; 2 Pet. 3:9). Keep in mind the prolonged and deliberate refusal by Pharaoh of every appeal made by God. Nothing changed his attitude nor brought him to a single thought of repentance. He was against God and against everyone and everything that belonged to God. That evil unbelief made judgement inevitable. It is a solemn theme. We have illustrations of how evil calls forth God's judgement in the story of the Flood (Gen. 6:5-7, 11-13); in the persistent corruption in the evil city of Sodom (Gen. 18:20-21); and in the building up of evil and its consequences spoken of by Jesus in Matthew 23:29-39. But we must not forget how Jesus wept over Jerusalem in Luke 13:34-35; 19:41-44. How willing he had been to gather the people to himself for salvation and life, but they refused. That was their considered choice. The choices unbelief makes will be exposed for what they are on the day of final judgement, as we read in Revelation 9:20-21. Between the sinner and his judgement there stands the Cross of Christ, but if that way of salvation is refused there is nothing left but judgement. The chapter is summarised in a very factual way in verse 30. That day, and in that way, the Lord saved Israel from the hands of the Egyptians.

A GREAT SONG

This is the beginning of the first song recorded in Scripture and it has to do with the testimony of a whole congregation in praise to the God who had saved and delivered them gloriously. The occasion was a celebration which may have gone on quite some time, because we are told in verses 20-21 that Miriam and the women's choir took up the theme in further song and dance, which was a natural way for these people to express themselves. There are no grounds in this one verse for introducing dance and drama into present-day worship. Note carefully how in this song of worship the emphasis is on the Person of God and his glorious activity in the salvation of his people. We must note also that this was not a 'new' God the people were singing about but the unchanging and unchangeable God of their fathers (Jas 1:17, AV). He and his salvation are the same yesterday, today and forever (Heb. 13:8). This is the God who always has been and always will be active on behalf of his people, the God who takes issue with the massed powers and persons of evil in order to deal with them. We may feel it is rather 'sub-Christian' to rejoice in this way at the defeat of the enemy because, after all, Jesus said we are to love our enemies (Matt. 5:44). Jesus' words have a personal and individual application and must not be used to prevent the challenging of and opposition to the powers of evil that ravage the world. The New Testament makes plain that we are called to spiritual warfare of the most basic kind (Eph. 6:10ff.). If we are ever called to face the full unmasked fury of evil, as many young and old in our world do face it, then we will understand the relief and thanksgiving expressed in this song of praise. God was being enthroned on the praises of his people (Ps. 22:3, NIV footnote).

15:4-12

A GREAT VICTORY

This is the history of what actually happened, recorded in poetry rather than prose. Poetic language does not mean it was not real. It was a tremendous experience for the Israelites, and they were in no doubt that their God had done great things for them because of which they were glad indeed (Ps. 126:1-3). The focus of the song is more upon God than upon the plight of the enemy. Their God had triumphed gloriously (v.1). The right hand of

God's power and authority had dealt with the enemy who had enslaved them (v.6). The great majesty of God (v.7) showed the proud pretensions of Pharaoh to be nothing at all. Evil likes to portray itself as strong, but it can never be a problem to God who deals with evil when the time is right and by the methods that are correct (Ps. 2:1-4). The Israelites saw that their God was the God of creation (v.8), and the picture of the waters obeying the command of God should make us think of the story in Mark 4:35-41 and the astonished comment of the disciples that even the wind and waves obeyed him. In Moses' song the two verses 9 and 10 show the proud, wilful self-confidence of the enemy and his merciless intentions to be truly pathetic. God simply blew with the breath of his mouth and they were finished. That is a comforting thought, especially when we read passages such as 2 Thessalonians 2:1-9 which speak of the eruption of evil into society in the last days. The reference to the majestic holiness of God in verse 11 reminds us how important it is to have right thoughts about God. It is true of so many of us that 'Your God is too small'. The holiness of God is an awesome concept, which can inspire a right fear, worship and trust.

A GREAT GOD

The constant theme of this song is the Person of God, who he is in his uniqueness, majesty and activity (vv.11, 12). It calls the people to consider the God with whom all have to deal. Read Habakkuk 2:20 and Zechariah 2:13 in the light of our tendency to consider all things in relation to people, their needs, hopes, expectations and rights. It is when we consider God that all other persons, things and issues begin to be seen in their true dimension and perspective. As Moses sang this song he reminded the people first of the Person of God (v.11), then what God had done (vv.12, 13), and finally what God was going to do (v.17). It must have thrilled both Moses and the people to express the glorious truth that their past, their present and their future were in the good and strong hand of their God. But it is not just the power of God to subdue the enemy and to protect his people that is the theme. There is God's personal interest, his steadfast love, the price he paid for their redemption (1 Pet. 1:18-20), and his guiding hand that leads his people to their destination. We need to think far more than we do about God's clear plans for his people: the Israelites in their day and us who believe in our day. We do well to ponder often God's statement in Jeremiah 29:11, especially when the way is dark and full of uncertainty.

We may be uncertain; God never is, and he is totally confident about the success of his purposes. The issues belong to him, and to him alone (Ps. 68:20, AV). Power belongs to him alone (Ps. 62:11, AV), and our times, with all their whys, whens and wheres are in his hands, and his hands alone (Ps. 31:15). Think of his steadfast love, and remember that there is nothing, human or demonic, known or unknown, present or future that has the power to separate us from that love (Rom. 8:38-39). Try to find and read Toplady's hymn, 'A Sovereign Protector I have, unseen, yet for ever at hand'.[11] That is what Moses was singing about.

15:13-21

A GREAT FUTURE

Read this final section of the song again in order to savour the thrill, comfort and assurance that Moses and the people had found in their recent experience. They were sobered as well as thrilled by the complete overthrow of their dread enemy, just when they thought they had no hope. They were already aware, as they looked ahead, that other enemies were having second thoughts about opposing and attacking them (v.15). But they were even more moved and thrilled by the thought of their God standing guard over them as they marched forward at his command (v.16). Could Paul have been thinking of occasions such as this when he wrote about the peace of God, which passes understanding, keeping guard over feelings and thoughts (Phil. 4:6, 7)? It is a conscious awareness of God that keeps us in peace (Isa. 26:3), but this requires the effort of faith. How often in Scripture we are urged to have faith in God and to trust him. After all, he knows what he is doing with us, for us and through us. It is God who reigns (v.18). And, as Moses reminds all of us, the sovereignty of God is not just a theological concept, but a practical reality in the ongoing experiences of life (vv.18, 19). It is little wonder that Miriam and the women sang and celebrated the wonderful works of God. There is no doubt that as the people sang together they encouraged one another and enabled one another to express to God their worship and thanksgiving. When we consider how often congregational praise is somewhat lifeless or even dreary; and when we consider the indifferent expression of many faces, we cannot but wonder if the people singing may in fact not know God, are not walking with God nor experiencing the touch of his gracious power in their lives. If God has done great things for us, and if he has been good to us, then the call certainly is, 'Stand up and bless the Lord, ye people of His choice; stand up and bless the Lord your God with heart and soul and voice.'[12]

FORGETFULNESS

The people had known the good hand of their God upon them in their deliverance from Pharaoh. They had rejoiced in their God, recognising his past mercies (v.13) and declaring their trust in him for the future (v.17). The thrill and excitement of the 'big' and 'special' occasion and experience were past and it was back to the ordinary in the forward march of obedience to their God. Within *three days* the complaining started. Of course for a desert journey with so many people and their flocks, water was a necessity. Did they carry no supply in water skins? Had they not thought of such preparation? Did they have any knowledge of the sites of the various oases, as we tend to know the sites of service stations on motorways? Had they not expected that the journey would be demanding? We cannot answer these questions but we can see just how quickly difficulty led to complaint and criticism. They had forgotten God's promises and his presence with them. They had forgotten all his wonderful deliverances. They had forgotten the significant and trustworthy leadership of Moses. They had forgotten their expressions of confidence in God. The one thing uppermost in their thoughts was their immediate discomfort and the possibility that it might get worse. It may have been that they expected their journey after the wonders of the Red Sea to be one long experience of thrill and victory. But when life is like that we learn indulgence and carelessness, we do not learn faith. This was indeed a testing of their faith. When they came to Marah they thought their problems were over. There was a well. There would be excitement and relief. But when they tasted the water it was bitter, and they felt it too much of a risk to drink it. They did not cry to God. They did not remember the God who had shown his power over the waters in Egypt's rivers and in the Red Sea. They turned their bitterness on their leader and in their murmuring and grumbling they exposed the shallowness of their faith. This raises questions about the spiritual reality of their hearty singing!

15:25-27

PRAYER IS THE ANSWER

We are not told anything of the disappointment, hurt and shock that Moses must have felt in this reaction of the people for whom he had done so much as their God-appointed leader. It is doubtful if the people even considered whether Moses had any human feelings. But Moses was a true servant of God and of God's people and he knew what to do. He went straight to God and cried to him in prayer. We are not told the content of Moses' prayer. It may simply have been, 'Lord, what shall I do?' Moses had not forgotten God's promised presence, and his prayer was answered instantly. We do not know what the tree or bush was but commentators suggest that certain aromatic shrubs had a flavour that would counteract the bitter taste of the water and make it palatable. Moses, having been a shepherd, may have known about such shrubs and needed only to be reminded by God that there was a 'natural' solution to the water problem. On the other hand, we do not in any sense seek to explain away the miracle element in the story. We should perhaps concentrate on the unhesitating obedience of Moses to what God told him to do. What we must also see is the astonishing goodness of God in his response to this discontented people. How true it is that where sin abounds, grace much more abounds (Rom. 5:20). If we want to draw a symbolic lesson from the event, we can do no better than think of how we sing about the Cross that 'sweetens every bitter cup'.[13] It is certainty true that God can make even the bitter experiences of life into sources of blessing beyond all expectation. Keep in mind that not much further on along the road by which God was leading them there were waiting, all ready, the twelve springs of fresh water at Elim. Never forget that our God is the Shepherd God who leads his flock to quiet waters and pastures of rest, even though the road may have dark valleys and real enemies. Read Psalm 23 and read it slowly so that familiarity does not steal away the blessing.

THE TEST OF FAITH

There is one final lesson to be learned from this passage and it is in verses 25-27. The experiences that come to God's people in their pilgrim journeys are many and varied and can be bitter as well as sweet. But we are taught here that all the experiences are opportunities for learning and they are also occasions when God tests the faith and the reality of his people. The reaction of the people in meeting the bitter water showed them to be shallow in their faith and obedience. They did not take time to consider their situation in the light of God's goodness and mercy, but instantly grumbled and complained. Through their difficulty, their wrong reaction, and his own answer to the crisis, God taught his people the basic lesson of the importance of the obedience of faith. Of course, if we are to listen to God we must be prepared to be still (Ps. 46:10), to check our instinctive reactions, and to wait upon him. There are different kinds of listening, and that is why Jesus said to take heed *how* we hear (Luke 8:18). There is a listening to the Word of

God, and a recognising of that Word that can be without faith and therefore without benefit. In verse 26 the emphasis is on listening to God, pleasing God, learning from God and obeying God. As early as this in their journey, the people were taught that blessing is dependent on obedience. But there is also great encouragement at the end of verse 26. God assured his people that he would not deal with them as he dealt with the Egyptians. He was the God of their salvation not the God of judgement. In Egypt's plagues the water was turned to blood, but here the bitter water was made sweet. God's redeemed people will not find the water God supplies to be unpalatable or inappropriate. After all, he is the God who heals his people of their many ailments, not least the 'diseases' of unbelief and disobedience. The operations of the Great Physician can be painful but his objective is always to make us whole (Job 5:17-18; Jer. 30:17).

16:1-3

SELF-CENTRED

Before we register shock at the Israelites grumbling again so soon and begin to criticise them, remember that the Bible is like a mirror in which we see ourselves (Jas 1:22-25). It is so easy to forget all the good we have received from God, from family and from congregation, when something happens that displeases us. It is quite staggering to think that only a month had elapsed since this people had been delivered from slavery in Egypt by the mighty power of God (Exod. 12:2, 6; 16:1). They had experienced the dividing of the sea, the judgement of their enemies, the sweetening of the bitter waters and the plentiful water of Elim. Now they were being led by their God, who is all-wise as well as all-powerful, to a land and a life of blessing beyond anything they could imagine, and certainly more than they ever deserved. Of course, the future held for them not just blessing but significant work in relation to the ongoing purposes of God and they had to be prepared for that. The wilderness journey was part of that preparation and they were being led in it and through it by God whose methods are always perfectly suited to the need and the objective. However, there seems to have been no thought among the people regarding their future *service*. Their concern was simply for their immediate situation and the focus of their thought and feeling was their own discomfort. What God wanted, what God was doing with them, for them and through them had become, if they thought of that at all, very secondary issues. The whole congregation, not just a few vocal discontents, murmured against Moses and Aaron. Their words reveal how this people who had been saved by God and who liked the benefits of salvation, were in fact a people whose motivation was self-pleasing and self-gratifying. Like Lot's wife (Gen. 19:24-26), the people looked back to the worldly way of life they once enjoyed. They made no mention of their slavery, their lack of freedom, their humiliation in these days. The lesson is practical. Before giving way to criticism, count your blessings and consider how you would feel if God sent you back to your old way of life.

16:4-8

GOD HEARS AND SPEAKS

ote how swiftly the Lord intervened and spoke. We are not told if Moses and Aaron had had time to pray about the situation. Sometimes the God-appointed leaders of the work are so blasted by waves of criticism and complaining that they can scarcely pray. This does not mean that their prayer life is shallow or defective, as the next chapter will make plain (Exod. 17:8-13). In this passage it is clear that God, knowing every detail and aspect of the situation exactly, as he always does, came at once to Moses' side with instructions as to how this situation was to be dealt with. Moses may well have been greatly amazed and even a little disappointed that God was to deal so gently with those who had been so bitterly critical. Very soon the people who had refused to trust God to provide for them would be eating the food God had given. But they had more to learn than just trust. God was to search their hearts to see if there was in them the grace of obedience (v.4). Saving faith and practical obedience go together, and what God has joined must not be put asunder. Jesus made it very plain that if we love him we will keep his commandments (John 14:15), and James made it equally clear that faith without works is no faith at all (Jas 2:17). Moses did not ask any questions as to how bread was to be rained from Heaven, and how there was to be a daily delivery. God is able to do what he says he will do, no matter how impossible it may appear (Rom. 4:18-21; Heb. 11:17-19). Detailed instructions were given as to the day-by-day gathering and regarding the sanctity of the seventh day, and all this was told to the people. But the people were also reminded that their sinful complaining was against God not against their leaders, and that God knew all about their evil words and thoughts (Heb. 4:12,13; Rom. 2:16; Ps. 44:21). We must never forget that we are dealing with God day by day.

GLORY COMES NEAR

e have seen in verses 4-8 that God was ready to act in grace towards his people, but at the same time he is totally realistic. There must have been a tremor of apprehension among the people when they were summoned by Aaron in verses 9-10 and that tremor must have deepened when, even as Aaron spoke, the glory of the Lord appeared in the cloud. This cloud seems to refer to the visible token of God's presence with his people, and according to Exodus 13:21-22 the cloud by day and the pillar of fire by night were constant evidences of the fact that their God was with them. If that is so, why did the people's faith fail? Why did they not look to God in time of need? Why were they not encouraged by his presence? When people are preoccupied with themselves even obvious things can disappear into the background. *We* have all God's promises and all the evidences of his blessing and sure purposes in our Bibles. But is it not the case that in times of difficulty we forget, we do not look to God, we do not read our Bibles, or if we read them we do not read in faith? Difficulty certainly reveals just how far on we are, or are not, spiritually. The people had already been told that in the morning they would see the glory of God (v.7) but that seems to have referred to the giving

of the manna by miraculous means. And in these verses it was not yet morning. Perhaps the people were being taught that they had to deal with the Person of God, the God who spoke to them, the God who wanted them for his own people. They had to learn to deal with God in terms of fellowship, faith and obedience and not just as the God who supplied their needs and kept them safe. We must never make God our servant. What do you think made most impression on the people in verse 12? Was it the promise of flesh and bread or was it a solemn awareness of God?

GOD'S PROVISIONS

In the evening, as God had said, the meat came in the form of quails, small birds which normally roosted at night in low bushes or on the ground. Commentators tell us that large flocks of quails would have been on flights of migration at that time of year and, exhausted at night time, would have been easy to catch. The flesh of these birds had been a delicacy in Egypt and this fact would not have gone unnoticed by the complaining Israelites. They may have considered this provision a natural one but the timing of the arrival of the birds takes it into the realm of miracle. The giving of the manna was beyond question miraculous and the people did not recognise nor understand what it was. Of course many times in what happens to us we do not, at first or even for a long time, recognise that God has answered our prayers. Sometimes God gives us what we cry out for and at other times he withholds it. But always he gives us what we need, and in the way he gives he is teaching us faith and dependence. At first the Israelites may not have been impressed with what God had given them (v.15). It was different from what they were accustomed to, different from what they had expected and there could well have been an attitude of reluctance or indifference. That kind of thing happens in churches when people do not get the kind of preaching, teaching or singing that they expect or want or have been accustomed to. What God gives is not always recognised and received as the right and best thing for our souls. Remember that the Israelites had already had in the evening the tasty quail meat and the manna may have seemed dull by comparison. But on the instructions of Moses, they set about gathering it. The ability to gather varied but, either by miracle or by a process of pooling the gathered manna and a sharing it out, everyone had a sufficient supply. It is a wonderful story, but a shadow is cast on it as we shall see.

THE UNSEEN ENEMY

We must keep in mind the spiritual lessons of the giving of the manna and this is emphasised in John 6:25-35 and 1 Corinthians 10:1-5. The story we are reading is that of God giving his people the bread of life, without which no-one can truly live (Deut. 8:1-3; Matt. 4:1-4). The people must have marvelled and been greatly relieved that God had met their need so swiftly and so fully. It was indeed an amazing spiritual experience. They had been guided and instructed with great care and told that God's provision was to be a day-by-day one, so that they would be encouraged to live looking to God, and to pray, 'Give us this day our daily bread.' But such is the perversity of unbelief that some of the people (we are not told how many) left some manna for the next day, no doubt saying, 'Just in case something goes wrong.' We must see in this whole chapter the work of Satan in his crafty deceiving of God's own people. It was the Devil who stirred their discontent. It was the Devil who made them forget God. It was the Devil who blinded them to the pillar of cloud and fire that symbolised God's presence and assured them of it. It was the Devil who inspired the stupid disobedience of those who in unbelief hoarded God's provision. It was the Devil who saw clearly that if he could get some to go wrong he would soon get others to follow. This emphasis on the Devil and his subtle devices (2 Cor. 2:11) is echoed in Jesus' parable about the good seed and the weeds in Matthew 13:24-30, 36-43. No-one noticed exactly when the enemy sowed his evil seed. It is the same in this story. Just exactly when the first stirrings of disobedience began we cannot tell. We need to watch as well as pray. It is little wonder that Moses was angry but we do not know how he expressed his anger, nor how the people reacted. The anger of a man described as the meekest man on earth should be an experience long to be remembered. The story will yet tell us that the people forgot very soon.

16:22-30

THE APPOINTED SABBATH

There are two lessons in this passage: the importance of the Sabbath day of rest from work and the persistence of the Israelites in their blind unbelief and disobedience. Keep in mind that we are still well before the giving of the Ten Commandments, in which God commanded the people to keep or preserve the Sabbath. But the principle had already been established. Long before the time of the giving of the manna, right from the time of creation, the day of rest from labour had been established. When

God had done all the work of creation he rested in his finished work (Gen. 2:1-3), and the emphasis of God's finished work undergirds the whole principle of Sabbath-keeping. When Jesus died for our sins and rose again on the first day of the new week, *his* work of salvation was completed, and on the first day of the week we now rest and keep the day holy, as a reminder to ourselves and to all the world that our faith rests in the finished work of Christ. The same principle is found in the story of the manna. God provided totally for his people's salvation and life, and in token of that full provision no gathering of manna was to take place on the Sabbath. Indeed the people were told that there would be no manna there to be gathered on the Sabbath. This day was to be kept for the Lord (v.23), and the people's keeping of it would be a token of their faith, commitment and obedience, and it would be a joy and pleasure to the Lord. Most of the people seem to have believed and obeyed and they proved the trustworthiness of their God (v.24). But some in a worldly attitude, refusing the spiritual teaching that came from God through Moses, went out to gather manna and found none. They seem to have had no conscience about their disobedience, and no doubt resented the displeasure expressed by God. But note that God said to Moses, 'How long will you refuse to keep my commands?' (v.28). This was not a personal rebuke to Moses who certainly would not himself have gathered on the Sabbath. It was a recognition that the people of God were one people, and as a people they had sinned. There would be tension among the people and even anger because some foolish and arrogant souls had led Israel astray, cf. Joshua 7:1-12.

16: 31 - 36

REMEMBER

Those who want to consider more fully the nature, the nutritional value, and the possible scientific side of the production of manna in relation to the evaporation of the dew (v.14) should consult a Bible Dictionary. The passage we have here must have been written later than the general narrative because reference is made to the Tabernacle (not yet constructed) and to the Ark of Testimony, the contents of which are referred to in Hebrews 9:1-5. We need not be distracted by the fact that manna, which went bad if kept overnight, was now to be kept in a jar throughout the generations. The manna, only now given, kept on being given for the forty years of Israel's journeys and wanderings, an interesting point that tells us that even in their wanderings of disobedience God still provided for his people. The emphasis in this fascinating postscript to the story of the manna is that of remembrance. At the heart of Israel's worship there was to be this reminder of God's bountiful provision for his people, sinners though they were. At the heart of Christian worship is the Communion Table of broken bread and poured out wine, a wonderful remembrance of the salvation God worked for his people at such infinite cost. This he did, sinners though we were, are, and will ever be. It was while we were sinners that Christ died for us (Rom. 5:6-8). But the Ark of Testimony also held the Tables of God's Law, a reminder along with the manna that it is God's living Word that is the bread on which our souls are fed. God's Word, like the manna, never changes and will never fail right through our journey. God's Spirit through God's Word always points us to the Saviour.

17:1-7

SELF-PITY

The people and work of God were moving forward at the command of God, in the will of God, in the company of God, into the future that God had promised and prepared for them. The astonishing thing is that whenever any difficulty arose, whenever anything seemed to threaten their comfort and satisfaction, they complained and their bitter criticism was always directed at their leader. We have seen this murmuring, complaining spirit in

Exodus 14:11, 12; 15:23, 24; 16:2-3; and again in this story. There seems to be no indication of the people ever expressing their gratitude to Moses or voicing any appreciation of his leadership. Now, when people speak only to complain and criticise, the situation is serious, because it indicates not just a shallow spirituality but a wrong attitude to *God*. This is made plain in the warning given to the people after their long wanderings in the wilderness when, at last, they were ready to go forward into the land of Canaan (Deut. 6:16; 9:22). The seriousness of the wrong attitude of the people is made plain in the fact that these lapses of faith are referred to in Hebrews 3:7-12, 16 and 1 Corinthians 10:1-7, 11. Unbelief is really a slander on the character of God. It suggests that God has not been true to his word, that he has given promises that he is not fulfilling. Twice in the passage (vv.2, 7) the nature of the people's complaint is described as putting God to the test. He had promised a life and destiny in a land of blessing, but where was it? They wanted the blessing and they wanted it immediately, and they wanted it without the cost and discipline of the journey. But that kind of spiritual life makes people flabby both morally and spiritually, a people not inclined for disciplined service. Perhaps the reason why we know little of the power of God in our lives and service is because we know little of the fellowship of his sufferings (Phil. 3:10).

GOD'S GREAT PATIENCE

This passage deserves fuller study. Was it accidental that there was no water? Had God chosen the wrong route for them or had he overlooked the need for water? Should the people not have been expecting to face thirst travelling through a desert? Had they expected the life of liberty and pilgrimage to be easy? When this difficulty arose did they not remember how on previous occasions of crisis God had met and supplied their need? Had they forgotten, as we so often forget, the fact of the great faithfulness of God (Lam. 3:22, 23) and the misery of their life of slavery before the salvation of God set them free? It seems from verse 3 that again they were remembering only the 'spicy' aspects of their life in the world of Egypt. The whole incident challenges our hearts in respect of giving thanks for all that God has done for us. Because of his great goodness we must set ourselves to trust him and to wait upon him when the way gets hard. Moses' attempt to direct the people's thoughts to God in verse 2 was wise and brave but it failed. The devastating effect on Moses is seen in verse 4. Think what might have happened to the people and to their future if their leader had 'cracked' under the pressure of discontented criticism. Think of how Jesus was attacked by Satan through one of his best friends who tried to turn him away from God's appointed and costly way of obedience (Matt. 16:21-23). Moses despaired of the people but God showed himself, as he so often does, as the longsuffering God, the God of endless patience with his people, even when they are stupid, rebellious and disaffected (Exod. 34:6; Ps. 86:15; 2 Pet. 3:15). He knew the background of this people and how they had gone through privations, sufferings and humiliations that had left their mark and warped their attitudes. Moses had lived in Pharaoh's court and then in the independence and freedom of his shepherd's life. God understood, made allowances, and without hesitation supplied the water the people needed. It is true that their faith would have become stronger if they had trusted. It is also true that we need to learn to understand why people react the way they do, then we will not despair of them.

17:8-16

AN OPENING FOR THE ENEMY

We concentrate on verse 8, which sets the context for the marvellous lesson that follows. The coming of the people of Amalek to fight against the Israelites can be thought of as the natural reaction of a people determined to protect their territory against the advancing hordes of strangers. It could also be seen as an example of God lifting his shield of protection from a people who had refused to trust him: God saying to unbelieving, discontented people to go it alone and see how they coped. We could see in Amalek an attack on God's work by Satan, who had been given the opportunity and opening by the spiritual disaffection of God's own people. Again, we could see the whole incident as an example of God's providential discipline and instruction. He had given his people deliverance, promises, encouragements, signs of his presence and in times of crisis had provided them with bread and water to meet their needs. Now God provided them with spiritual warfare so that they might have opportunity to learn spiritual priorities and to reaffirm their spiritual commitment. Whether in personal life or congregational life there is nothing like a crisis and danger to get God's people to be realistic and to recognise that there are issues far more important than personal comfort and fulfilment. Someone has said that tribulations are God's gracious gifts to help us on to glory. That is quite a thought! It is interesting that in this whole passage there is no suggestion of any criticism of Moses, no hesitation about accepting his leadership and obeying his instructions. Keep in mind that the Israelites had already had experience of God dealing with dangerous attacks when he dealt with Pharaoh's armies (Exod. 14:10, 19-20, 26-28). This attack was a danger that threatened their future. In our Christian service we must always have an eye to the future. God's work is long-term and just as we have inherited the work from those who went before us, so others will inherit from us. We must see to it that we leave our children a spiritual inheritance that is true.

PRAYER

Moses showed his spiritual leadership by recognising at once the real nature of the attack. It was a spiritual battle not a merely human one, and the weapons of that kind of warfare are not worldly (2 Cor. 10:3-4). The practical down-to-earth matters had to be organised and Joshua, the soldier, was instructed to attend to that. Moses made plain that he would not go with the soldiers, because there was another battle to be fought, the battle of prayer, on which the whole issue would depend. We do not know if Moses and his colleagues were visible to the soldiers on the battlefield. He may have been forgotten in the hard business of the fight or even criticised by some for not being amongst the fighting men: 'He's never there when there is real danger.' The truth was that Moses, Aaron and Hur were at the vital heart of the conflict. As prayer prevailed, so the battle went Israel's way, and as prayer slackened so the enemy began to advance. This is a lesson individual Christians and churches need to learn. When prayer is neglected, or is sidelined by other activities, or is left to the faithful few while others do 'more interesting' things, then the enemy of God and the gospel makes significant inroads. Why is the world so indifferent to the church? Why does the church seem so ineffective, making such little impact and bringing so few to saving faith? Is it because the church will do almost anything and everything except give itself to prayer and the ministry of the Word (Acts 6:1-4)? Neither the battle on the plain nor the spiritual battle on top of the hill was a brief encounter. It was sustained warfare and as it went on we are told that Moses the intercessor was worn out by exhaustion. Prayer is hard work and a spiritual battle. Moses could not have coped on his own. Aaron and Hur were there to share the costly work of intercession. They did not take over from Moses but, seeing the need, they were actually there with him, not just with him in spirit. They had to be there in person. Moses, mighty and trusted man of God as he was, needed them there, knew he needed them and right from the start took them with him. The Saviour did the same when he took Peter, James and John with him to Gethsemane and asked them to watch with him (Matt. 26:36-46). They failed. They fell asleep. What would have happened if Aaron and Hur had been 'out of sorts' spiritually, or if they had declined to share with their leader this spiritual battle even though he had asked them to be his prayer partners? How the church in our day needs to learn afresh that the church at prayer is the church really getting to grips with evangelism! Prayer *is* evangelism shorn of all its carnal attractions.

FAMILY TENSIONS

There has been no mention of Moses' wife and children since Exodus 4:18-26 and we learn here that they had been sent back to live with Jethro. Why they had been sent back is not clear. Moses' wife may have been out of sympathy with his commitment to the call of God. It may have been in anger that Moses sent his family away or it may have been for their safety in what was going to be a dangerous confrontation with Pharaoh. Perhaps Moses felt he would have more freedom to handle the work God had committed to him without the immediate responsibility of family matters. This does not mean in any sense that married men should neglect wives and children because they are so involved in the Lord's work. It is sad that many families feel neglected in this way and it is not surprising if such children grow up with a resentment against the church or even against

God. The arrival of Jethro with his daughter and her children is a reminder that Moses, in and through the significant and costly service we have been studying, was without his human family. We forget that many of God's mighty men knew a great deal about aloneness and indeed loneliness. Jesus knew the solitariness of being out front as the Servant of God's people. Paul testified that at one time of real need no-one stood with him (2 Tim. 4:16). We see the same in the life of Abraham, not least when he stood alone in God's presence in prayer for his nephew Lot (Gen. 18:22). Spurgeon said, 'There is no loneliness like that of a soul that has outstripped its fellows.' In typical eastern custom Jethro and Moses greeted each other with great politeness. They proceeded to discuss the past years and God's dealings with them. Note the thrill of verse 1. What God had been doing for the salvation of his people had become known far and wide. After all, God does not work in a secret corner (Acts 26:26) and, where God works, the Holy Spirit sees to it that the witness spreads. Think of how it is recorded in the Gospel that Jesus could not be hid (Mark 7:24). Jethro (having heard of God's dealings with the Israelites) was constrained to visit Moses, interested and impressed but perhaps not yet fully persuaded in terms of personal faith. Then Moses told in detail the story of God's great work of salvation for his people, and Jethro responded with words that seem beyond question to express a personal faith. There is no mention of what Zipporah was thinking. The fact that neither wife nor sons feature in the development of the story may suggest that when Jethro left (18:27) his daughter and grandchildren went with him.

18:13-23

POTENTIAL BURN-OUT

e have emphasised the very human side of the story but we must also see the sovereign providence of God in the arrival of Jethro at this particular stage. That great demands had been made on Moses is obvious. There had been a series of crises which had called for a tremendous expenditure of spiritual energy and it is natural to feel tired. But the work had a long way to go yet and Moses had to be kept in a useable condition. The risk of 'burn-out' had to be avoided. Some means had to be found so that Moses could stand in God's presence for the people, assured that other responsibilities were being rightly looked after. It was Jethro, coming from outside the actual situation, who saw the need for help if Moses was not to be worn out prematurely. God had his servant prepared and brought him into the situation. In addition to his spiritual leadership and his ministry of intercession Moses also

had an ongoing, very demanding work of counselling. When Jethro had had time to observe, it was clear to him that this kind of work-load was more than any one man could carry long-term, and he gave advice which Moses accepted (v.24). Some people say Moses made a basic mistake in that he listened to the advice of a relative rather than listening to God. That can be an area of danger and we must guard against accepting people and their advice in spiritual issues simply because we like them. Friends and family can be wrong, as they were in the case of Jesus in Mark 3:20, 21. We must be careful about how we respond to advice, especially from those who unexpectedly come into our situation. But it is clear from verse 23 that Jethro had no desire to usurp Moses' spiritual leadership, and both he and Moses desired only the wise will of God. Moses, being the kind of spiritual man we have seen him to be, seems to have pondered Jethro's advice, taking it to God in prayer. After due consideration he recognised that God had in fact given him guidance regarding the effective stewardship of his time and energy in the interest of both the people and the work. In verses 13-16 we are shown the pastoral and administrative burden Moses carried. He pointed out to Jethro that the need was there and was genuine and pressing. But 'the need does not constitute the call' and, while everyone no doubt wanted Moses' personal help and counsel, there were needs that could quite well be met by others. The burden had to be shared. The question remains to this day: who ministers to ministers? Jethro, who did not really belong to the congregation, ministered to Moses. He was the only one who seemed to notice the need.

18:24-27

SHARING THE LOAD

The first priority in the life of every minister is to represent the people and their needs in Gods presence. Prayer is his first priority. Then he is to teach the people the truth of God in such a way that they learn how to live to please God. If either of these priorities is displaced, no matter how Christian and spiritual the things are that have demanded attention, then the minister is straying from his God-given calling. It is indeed a high and holy and demanding calling, and it was a wise old Christian woman who said to a minister, 'You cannot do all the preaching and all the praying.' She then covenanted to pray for that minister daily in respect of all his work. Jethro's advice was that Moses should choose and appoint spiritually minded men to be his partners in sharing the burden of work. This was the pattern adopted in the apostolic church as recorded in Acts 6:1-6, where godly men were set apart for God's work, not in terms of preaching, but to attend to a whole range of necessary work in order that the apostles might be free to be ministers of God's Word. Those who are eager to preach but not to do the less obvious work should remember that those who preach and teach are judged with more stringent judgement than others (Jas 3:1). Note the qualifications of the men to be chosen as Moses' partners: men of ability who had proved themselves, God-fearing men, trustworthy and dependable, who could not be bribed or manipulated (v.21). That means men whose desire was above all to please and honour God, men who could hold office without becoming proud. These were the kind of servants a congregation could trust. Such men would never seek to displace Moses, and they would recognise clearly those matters that needed to be told to Moses. The appointment of these elders, in the pattern of 1 Peter 5:1-4, was a good thing for the leading and guarding of the work of God as it went forward.

19:1-6

APPOINTMENT WITH GOD

On a particular day in the third month after they had left Egypt the Israelites came to *the* mountain in the wilderness of Sinai. This was the very place where God had revealed himself to Moses and where the promise had been given that God would meet him at that mountain (Exod. 3:1, 12). They were to meet with their God (v.17), and there was, understandably, a feeling of apprehension (v.16). Of course, this was not a terminus, but it was a very significant stage. There is something wonderfully simple and yet quite awesome in the statement that Moses went up to God and God spoke with him (v.3). Moses seems to have known he had this appointment with God. There was not the fear and hesitation he had shown at the burning bush (Exod. 3:11; 4:10) and we should perhaps see here signs of the beginning and development of the relationship God had with Moses, expressed so beautifully in Exodus 33:11. The message Moses was given to speak to the people was a wonderful one. They were to remember all God had done for them and how he had dealt with them. God had brought them to himself (v.4) because he wanted them to be his people, a people with whom he would enjoy fellowship. This is the theme taken up in 1 Peter 2:9, 10. In spite of all their sins, failures, disobedience and complaining criticism, God still wanted them and would not give them up (Hos. 11:7-9). He will bear them on eagle's wings (v.4; cf. Deut. 32:10-11). This may be a reference to the eagle disturbing the nest and so forcing the young to fly, but watching over them ready to catch them when necessary. Perhaps even more the reference is to the eagle's effortless soaring to the heights. It seems to have no difficulty, and so it is with

God. But not only so, God carries his people to the heights with him. There is simply no limit to the possibilities, but these possibilities call for the obedience of faith. Obedience is not a condition of the making of the covenant. God had already committed himself to his people in sovereign grace. The covenant stands, but the enjoyment and blessing of it come only with obedience. The first blessing is that of fellowship with God, the gracious companionship that warms the heart and blesses the life (Luke 24:32; 1 John 1:3, 7). God wants us, loves us and enjoys us personally, but it is in company with others not in detached individuality that we enjoy God and serve him. We are to be a kingdom of priests, all related, inter-dependent, and organised with free access to God at any time, serving God in terms of worship, praise and thanksgiving. In this way we become a distinct people, set apart for God to be his witnesses and servants in the world, channels of his grace to needy people.

19:7-15

CONSECRATION

The people seem to have sensed the importance of the occasion. They may have had a real awareness of the near presence of God, and they certainly grasped the significance of the blessings that were being promised them. Their response was immediate and enthusiastic. In the atmosphere of the 'big occasion' they heard the call to commitment and consecration, and, while we may have doubts about the depth of their response, it appears that God took them at their word. Moses was then commanded to go and tell the people to prepare themselves to meet with God, because God was in fact coming to meet with them and to speak to them. As they heard Moses' instructions the people may well have had second thoughts about their enthusiastic words of commitment (v.8). The first requirement of preparation to deal with God was to be personal sanctification. This is the significance of the washing in verse 10. Of course, this required the people to recognise that they were sinners and needed cleansing, and a spirit of enthusiasm for God does not always have this element (read Psalm 51:1-12 and 1 John 1:8-10). The second element of preparation was to set a guard against spiritual presumption (vv.12-13). A spirit of enthusiasm can so easily lead to a spirit of familiarity with God, which can cause people to barge into God's presence, forgetting that he is holy and that there is a need for reverence and godly fear. The final element in preparation in verse 15 indicates that at times, in the interest of dealing with God in respect of future service, there is a need to abstain from what is basically natural, right and permitted. God's service takes precedence over all our rights to personal fulfilment. That this should not be taken to extremes by unwise spirituality is made clear in 1 Corinthians 7:5. In today's passage (vv.12-13) there may be an indication that some would regard these standards of preparation as extreme and unnecessary. That attitude was to be seen as defiance of God and dealt with accordingly.

19:16- 25

A HOLY GOD

On the third day, as he had promised, God manifested himself in a way that brought a spirit of awe and trembling upon the people: fire, cloud, thunder, smoke and a quaking of the mountain. Why did God manifest himself in this way? He had already made himself known as the God who saves, keeps, guards, blesses and provides with tender care for his people. But there was something more that the people (and we) must learn about God and it is in no sense a contradiction of his wonderful love. God is love (1 John 4:16), but he is also holy and dwells in light no-one can approach (1 Tim. 6:16); and is of purer eyes than to look on evil or tolerate wrong (Hab. 1:13). Read Isaiah 6:1-5, Daniel 10:2-9 and Revelation 1:12-18, passages which describe in plainest of terms the holiness of God.

In Hebrews 12:18-21, 25, 29, where the occasion at Sinai is referred to, God is spoken of as a consuming fire. We are right to sing in worship, 'Holy, holy, holy, Lord God Almighty',[14] and,

> Eternal light! Eternal light!
> How pure the soul must be,
> When, placed within Thy searching sight,
> It shrinks not, but, with calm delight,
> Can live, and look on Thee.[15]

It is only because this holy God spared not his own Son but delivered him up for our salvation that we can come to him and live in him. We need to learn afresh what it is to worship and to bow down before God. Read Habakkuk 2:20 and Zechariah 2:13. This is the God with whom we have to do.

19:1-25

BE CAREFUL!

Before leaving this chapter take note of how Moses went backwards and forwards between God and the people. It was to Moses that God spoke and this may have been, in measure, a rebuke to the people who had so often refused to recognise him as God's appointed leader and spokesman. God was making it very clear that he trusted Moses. We may think of the great privilege given to Moses to have such access to God and such personal conversations with God, but at the same time we must think of the immense spiritual responsibility that this privilege brought. To stand in the presence of the majesty of God, to be his ambassador, and to be the intermediary between God and his people is indeed an awesome calling. We also need to take note of how God, who sees and knows the secret thoughts of people's hearts far better than his servants do, instructed Moses to go down and warn the people *again* not to come near the mountain (vv.21-23). Curiosity about and fascination with signs and wonders in the spiritual realm can cause people to forget all God has said, and to intrude into realms where they have no right to be and which can prove dangerous. There may also be a suggestion here that the priests (it is not clear who they were but the reference may be to the elders or heads of families) may have resented the fact that only Moses was being given this very important ministry in the sight of the people. Spiritual jealousy can be powerful and dangerous and can cause Christian men and women to intrude into areas of service where they have not been called to be. Experience testifies to the fact that even on the holiest of occasions spiritual pride can rear its ugly head. Think of James, John and their mother in Mark 10:35-37 and of how all the disciples argued about place and prominence in Mark 9:33-35. In due time Moses would face a similar spiritual intrusion, recorded in Numbers 12:1-2. It is sad that Aaron, the man who was called to give Moses the support and fellowship he needed, proved later to be such a sore disappointment (Exod. 32:1-6).

THE GOD OF THE COMMANDMENTS

The Ten Commandments are not the product of human reasoning. They were given by God to his people with the clear objective of keeping them from sin (Exod. 20:20), and to enable them to live lives pleasing to him, lives that could be used in his service. Seen in this context we recognise the Commandments to be words of grace rather than laws of condemnation. This is confirmed by God's description of himself as the God who, in sovereign grace, had redeemed and saved his people, bringing them out of the land of Egypt into a life of liberty, hope and destiny. It is important to recognise the fact that God's grace came and was operative before God's Law. The Commandments were not given in the Garden of Eden before or immediately after the Fall; at the time of the Flood; at the call of Abraham; nor for four hundred years after Abraham. Before the Law was ever given men and women found the way of salvation which is by faith not by the works of human striving to keep God's Law(Rom. 3:19-26). Why then did God give his Commandments at this time? The Law was given in relation to the fact of sin (Gal. 3:19), and it is by the Law that the knowledge of sin presses home in conviction to the hearts of sinners. But the Law can only convict, it cannot save, and its function is to persuade us all that if we are to live to please God then we need a Saviour (Gal. 3:23-24). The Ten Commandments are indeed, in their prescriptions and prohibitions, ten words of grace and they do not belong only to the Old Testament. God's Law must not be swept aside. Jesus said so in Matthew 5:17-20 and he went on to set the standard even higher (Matt. 5:21-37). Jesus also said that if we love him we will keep his commandments (John 14:15, 21, 23-24). To do this we need to know and understand them and for that reason we study them one by one.

20:3

NO OTHER GODS

The first four commandments deal with our relationship to God and the other six deal with our relationship with others. This division is neither accidental nor incidental, because it is as we are right with God that we will have the desire, the motivation and the capacity to do right by others, and to deal rightly with the service God has called us to. As the children of Israel prepared to go forward into what God had marked out for them, God gave this first commandment: you shall have no other gods before *Me*, or besides *Me*, or alongside *Me*. This means more than just 'God first' in every aspect of life. The Israelites, like ourselves, lived and worked in a pluralistic society in which people thought of, worshipped and sacrificed to, a whole host of 'gods': territorial gods, nature gods, gods at war with each other and even 'unknown gods' (Acts 17:22-23). Some worshipped gods of wood and stone, unaware that often behind these idols there were spirits which were evil, spirits which they neither understood nor could control (1 Cor. 8:1-7; 10:14-21). In our day some worship the State, the Party, Sport, Fitness, Pleasure or Sex. These are the things that really matter to them and to which they are prepared to give time and energy. But all these 'gods' bring people into bondage not freedom. Israel was reminded that their God was the God who had redeemed and delivered them, opening the gates of freedom. What did they need of any other spurious god? The first commandment demands that we recognise that God alone is God; that we must let him be what he has revealed himself to be in Scripture and supremely in Jesus Christ. Read Isaiah 40:18-31. Is there any God like him? This is the God who gave his Son for our salvation and who, in him, gives us all we need, and from whose redeeming love we cannot be separated (Rom. 8:31-39). This commandment is given to save us from the folly of turning away from the God who saves to any other god who neither cares nor helps.

NO IDOLS

We must worship God on the basis of what he has revealed himself to be, and not as we may like to think or imagine him to be. It is part of the fallenness of human nature to create 'images' or 'imaginations' of God, and in doing so there is an inevitable degeneration in the concept of God. This is made clear in Romans 1:18-23, and, as that chapter goes on to make plain, defective ideas about God lead to increasingly defective behaviour. That means the second commandment is a very practical one. If in our thinking we have an 'image' of God it will necessarily be limited to the scope and capacity of our intellect, which will of course reduce God to a 'size' we can handle and manipulate. In that process *we* are taking the place of God. In the account of the giving of the commandments recorded in Deuteronomy 4:12 the people heard God speak but saw no form, emphasising that they and we are taught to live by what God has said not by what we imagine. Jesus told his disciples that if they had seen him they had seen God the Father (John 14:8-9; cf. Heb. 1:1-3). In the Gospels the stories of Jesus give a variety of glimpses of what God is like. But always we must go to the whole Bible, comparing Scripture with Scripture, lest we take one aspect of God and build it into the whole picture. It is easy to sentimentalise our idea of God, and sentiment is not a help in the real demands of life. Another danger in images, even very spiritual ones, is that they become the focus of attention and distract from God himself, who is jealous in the sense that he wants us for himself. The realism of verses 5b-6 is startling but it reminds us that the world has been created by God in such a way that there is an inevitable entail or consequence of both evil and good in human lives. People are glad to accept that God loves even the sinner, but are reluctant to accept that God also rebukes, deals with and judges evil. We need to make sure we are believing in the real God.

GOD'S NAME

This is a necessary commandment in our day when the names of God and Jesus are used so casually, often as swear words. This is blasphemy and we are given a solemn reminder that God will not hold as guiltless those who sin in this respect. The 'name' in Hebrew thought is closely identified with the person and character of the one named. This means that those who use the name of God casually are people who have no real respect for God, for who he is and for what he has done. It is a significant indication of the sub-Christian and anti-Christian attitude of our modern society that people of all classes, including those prominent in public life, have no hesitation in abusing and blaspheming the name of Jesus and of God. They would never dare speak in such a disrespectful way of Allah lest they enraged the Muslim community. It is, and should be, very grieving to all Christians that there is so much wrong use of God's name. Of course, we have great opportunity to bear witness to our faith in all sorts of situations by simply and politely asking people not to be disrespectful to the One in whom we believe, whom we love and serve. Taking God's name in vain may also have specific reference to the taking of vows or oaths, whether vows in a court of law, or marriage vows, or vows of church membership. The same is true regarding the vows we make when singing certain hymns. If we do not really mean what we are saying, or if in the very process of saying the words we are making reservations regarding our lives and activities, then we are taking God's name in vain. Similarly, thoughtless repetition of Jesus' name in casual singing is unworthy and certainly is not worship. Sometimes in conversation we refer to 'the Lord' in a way that is almost casual, as if he was simply 'one of the boys'. 'Hallowed be thy name' is a primary petition in the Lord's prayer. Jesus challenged some people about using his name and giving the impression of being spiritual while living in disobedience (Luke 6:46; Matt. 7:21-23). There are also those who make use of the name of Jesus as if he belonged to them so that they might do miracles just like Jesus (Acts 19:13-17). We must be very careful how we use the holy name. Remember, God has said he will not hold people guiltless who sin with regard to his name.

20:8-11

GOD'S SABBATH

If we keep in mind that the Commandments are essentially words of grace from God, given for the blessing and guidance of all people in all generations, then we will begin to see the value, the benefit and the necessity of the fourth commandment concerning the Sabbath. We are told to remember the Sabbath and to keep it holy because that is exactly what it is, a day set apart and sanctified by God for the blessing of his people. When the work of creation was first completed God rested on the seventh day (Gen. 2:1-3). That means the pattern of a special day of rest has been built in to the fabric of creation by God himself. This commandment carries the same authority as the first three and the six that follow. The Sabbath was instituted by God as a day to rest in, to rejoice in, and to draw all the blessings from a work completed. In the same way now, in the Christian era, we keep the first day of the week, resting in and rejoicing in the finished work of our Lord Jesus Christ in his atoning death and glorious resurrection. It is this that makes Sunday a positive and enjoyable day, and those who find it dull and burdensome are really saying they do not know and have not tasted the glorious salvation God has accomplished in his Son Jesus Christ. Increasingly in a secular society Christian believers have a glorious opportunity to bear witness to the gospel and to create openings for conversation and discussion by the way they behave on a Sunday, what they do and refuse to do. Of course, it must be a way of life motivated by response to God's love and not just mere legal tradition. Christians must see to it that in what they regularly allow themselves to do on God's Day they do not contradict the holiness of the day. Of course there are works of necessity and mercy that have to be carried out on a Sunday. Jesus made that plain (Matt. 12:9-13). Ordinary work and shopping do not honour God, but going to church, twice where possible, carrying your Bible in your hand, is the kind of witness that makes worldly people blink in surprise. It may prod the conscience of some careless church members, but some may smile in mockery. If we do not use the Lord's Day properly it will diminish our blessing, cloud our witness, and will grieve God. Read Isaiah 58:1-14. Read also Exodus 16:22-30 where we see again that before the Commandments were given the Sabbath was instituted, and those who chose to ignore God's command discovered their folly. The BBC radio programme, *Thought for the Day*, spoken on one occasion by a Jew had these words: 'Israel did not keep the Sabbath; the Sabbath kept Israel.' That is worth thinking about.

20:12

FATHERS AND MOTHERS

The second section of the commandments deals with social responsibilities and these begin in the home. Without doubt the pattern of behaviour learned and expressed in the home will be a great influence on how people deal with others in the wider areas of society. This fifth Commandment is stated more fully in Deuteronomy 5:16 and is referred to by Paul in Ephesians 6:1-4 and Colossians 3:20-21 in terms of obedience to parents. But we must not apply this command only to children and young people because it applies to the whole range of family relationships. There are adults who show remarkably little interest in and respect for their aged parents, and this is significant. We must note that the command is to honour and that may not always involve obedience. Little children should do as their parents command them but the parents must be wise, balanced, fair and consistent in the standards they set and the obedience they expect. As children grow older, the expression of this honouring has to change and parents must recognise this, especially when young people reach an age of maturity. Even more, when adult children get married, fathers and mothers have to recognise and accept that a new situation and a new relationship now exist. Sometimes children have to honour their parents by refusing to conform to an arbitrary pattern. Sometimes Christian children have to honour parents who are not believers by standing graciously but firmly in their faith and commitment to Christ and his service. To do otherwise would suggest to parents that faith and obedience were not really the most important things in life. There would be no witness to Jesus, and to withhold that from parents would not be honouring them. The blessing promised in this commandment has more to do with the welfare of the whole nation than with personal benefit, but no-one would deny that right relationships within the home are a blessing and benefit beyond calculation. The disappearance of true home life in our generation has a great deal to do with the disintegration of society. In the list of sins that corrupt and destroy society, disobedience to parents is included (Rom. 1:26-31; 2 Tim. 3:1-5). Of course it is easier for young people to treat older people with respect and care when they themselves have been treated in the same way. All relationships have to be governed and inspired by the fact that God has set immense value on each individual.

20:13

NO MURDER

The sixth commandment in its stark simplicity has to do with the sanctity of life. But that statement raises all sorts of questions about capital punishment, war, pacifism, abortion and euthanasia. If we take the commandment in an absolute and unqualified sense, we would have to adopt the attitude of Buddhists and refuse to kill plague-bearing insects and rabid dogs. In a fallen and disordered world in which evil works all manner of things contrary to God and all kinds of hurt and devastation to people, how is this commandment to be understood? It does not help to translate it, 'You shall not murder', because we would still have to define both killing and murder. When we move into the following chapters we will find that in elaborating the Law in its application to specific situations, the death penalty is spoken of, and distinctions are made between deliberate killing and unintentional killing. In Romans 13:1-5 there is reference to the God-given authority of the state to exercise judicial punishment and even execution. In 1 John 3:15 we are told that no murderer has eternal life, and that speaks of punishment even more severe than execution. In the world in which we live, sin is an intrusion, and when sin runs its devastating course it produces death from which no-one escapes (Jas 1:15). The most familiar verse in the Bible, John 3:16, speaks of the possibility of perishing and that is a solemn judgement pronounced by God. The subject is vast and we must keep in mind that basically punishment, to be justified, must be in terms of retribution: that is, it is deserved because of what has been done. To punish just in order to reform (compulsory cure) or to deter others (punish one to help someone else) cannot really be justified. Have we strayed from the wording of the commandment? We can kill by reckless driving, by shutting our eyes to drug-pushing, by introducing vulnerable people to alcohol, and we can kill a person's character and hope by careless and malicious gossip. By cruel attitudes and deliberate neglect we can drive someone to a slow death. The commandment, 'You shall not kill', demands that we do all in our power to preserve the sanctity of life.

NO SEXUAL SIN

The thoughts of not killing or destroying lead right on to this commandment which deals with the purity and sanctity of relationships, particularly the marriage relationship, the security of the home and family, and the well-being of children. We take this commandment as referring to all breaches of chastity and purity inside or outside the marriage bond. Sexual immorality limits the development of a relationship to the physical level and does not lead to people getting to know each other better. We cannot here discuss exactly what constitutes marriage, nor what are legitimate grounds for divorce, nor the question of remarriage after divorce. We emphasise that fallen men and women, left to themselves, will destroy themselves and all they come in contact with. Consider the devastation of society as a result of the free and easy attitude to sexual relations in our own day. Think of teenage pregnancies, the massive increase in divorce, children who do not really know who their parents are or which family they belong to. Read Jesus' words in Matthew 19:4-6, which emphasise that the right and natural pattern of sexual relationships, from the beginning of creation, is in life-long marriage. When people are faced with this commandment they resent it and say, 'Why not?' They insist on their 'rights', which are really their desires and their inclinations. But sexual sin is not a light thing, and the Bible is prepared to speak with plain words. Read 1 Corinthians 6:15-20 and mark the counsel, 'Flee from immorality.' Read Ephesians 5:3-6 and note the statement that God acts in anger against such sexual sins (Heb. 13:4). People tend to excuse or justify their adultery by saying that they were 'in love', but if one party was already married they had no right to 'fall in love'. They may have had strong feelings but they had no right to act on them. Stealing what belongs to another is involved in adultery; and so is false witness because often the words 'I love you' really mean 'I love me and I want you'. God's commandments search, challenge and condemn us, but there is hope in the gospel. In 1 Corinthians 6:9-11 Paul gives a list of ugly sins and says, 'And that is what some of you were. But you were washed'; washed clean by the power of the precious blood of Jesus Christ the Saviour (1 John 1:9).

NO STEALING

Stealing of any and every kind is forbidden absolutely. Stealing is taking what rightly belongs to someone else. We can steal from people and from God. If we come to church, jaded in spirit, having neglected God the whole week and we offer half-hearted praise and listen to his Word almost indifferently, then we are stealing from God the worship in spirit and in truth that is his right. We may not try to rob a bank, but we steal from the government what they legitimately require of us if we are dishonest in our Tax Returns (Matt. 22:15-22). When we speed in our cars we steal from people their right to go about the roads safely. If we pass on tittle-tattle or gossip (whether it is true or false) we can steal someone's reputation and their peace of mind. We can steal someone's friend, not always because we want that friend for ourselves but because we want to hurt the other person. This commandment recognises that things can legitimately belong to certain people, that is, the right of property is established and defended. It is right to own things if they are gained by honest toil or by free gift. But we have no right if we steal or gain by fraudulent means. The heart of stealing is greed and the motivation of greed is 'self', which can be ruthless in its desiring, ignoring any and every effect it might have on others.

The commandment that forbids stealing applies to companies and to the State as much as it applies to individuals. Think of the story of how King Ahab (the government) stole another man's vineyard and how God was angry (1 Kings 21:1-19). The ethics of the political and business worlds have to be kept under close scrutiny if this commandment is not to be broken. Of course, possessions bring problems, partly because we become attached to them, want more of them, and can be distracted from Christian service because of them. The *love* of money (not the possession of it) is the source of all kinds of evil (1 Tim. 6:10). Jesus told of a competent businessman who, legitimately as far as we can tell, prospered so greatly that he became so engrossed in the business of success that he forgot God and lost his soul (Luke 12:13-21). It is indeed hard for those who have riches to enter the Kingdom of God (Luke 18:24). Those who are rich have the privilege and the duty of ministering to others and to the work of the gospel. Read the story in Luke 16:19-31 and see how an affluent life-style can so dehumanise a person that there are eternal consequences. A safeguard is to remember that the first tithe of time, talents and money belongs to God by right, and stealing is forbidden (Mal. 3:8-9). Stewardship is a duty.

NO LIES

When we study the Commandments in sequence we see that every aspect of life, individual and social, is dealt with. Both the positive and negative commandments are given to guard us in areas in which our fallen human natures can so easily come to grief. God knows what we are like and what we are capable of, given the temptation and the opportunity at the same time. He sets the warning notices for our safety, our blessing and our preservation from the evil that would destroy us. In verses 12-15 the family, nuclear and social, is safeguarded, as are people's persons, relationships and property. Now in verse 16 a person's character, the honour of his name, is guarded. Shakespeare's words are apt:

> Who steals my purse, steals trash;
>
> ...
>
> But he that filches from me my good name
> Robs me of that which not enriches him,
> And makes me poor indeed.[16]

The word 'against' your neighbour makes plain that we are dealing here with words, suggestions, actions and attitudes which are used deliberately in a way that is false with the intention of causing hurt. Of course at times we say, 'I did not mean to cause trouble.' But we should have been more careful. During the 1939-45 war there were posters displaying the message, 'Careless talk costs lives.' We are not dealing in this commandment with the grievous sin of breaking confidence (although on an isolated occasion that may be necessary to prevent a disaster) but with the uncontrolled tongue, which can do endless harm and can be the instrument of Hell. Read James 3:1-12; Ephesians 4:29; Colossians 3:8-9; Psalm 55:21. When we know something and are tempted to pass it on, pause and ask, 'Is it true to say it? Is it necessary to say it? Is it kind to say it?' Why do we sometimes still say it? One further application of this commandment is indicated by Isaiah 29:13a. It is so easy to say and to sing all the right words without meaning them. How we need to make sure that our words and the pattern of our lives give the same message, and that the message is true.

20:17

NO COVETING

This commandment is given to curb and contradict the spirit of craving that can take possession of people's lives and drive them to destruction. Coveting is the spirit that can never really be satisfied, because the more it gets the more it wants. Even if life is surfeited with every conceivable thing, the person sees another having something he or she does not have, and to get that thing becomes the total obsession of life, and a whole family can be destroyed in the coveting of it. Of course, for various reasons of self-interest a man may not actually go after the thing or person he covets, but he is not thereby innocent. The Bible says that a man is as he thinks in his heart (Prov. 23:7, AV; Matt. 15:11, 15-20). It is not wrong to want good things, to want to be happy, to want to get on in a career and to want to be useful and fruitful in Christian life and service. Wanting to be one's best for God is commended in Jesus' parables in Matthew 13:44-46; 25:14-30. The problem arises when we begin to compare our situation with that of others. We then begin to forget and to devalue all that God has given us. We forget to give thanks to God and to those through whom God has ministered to us, and we become discontented. That is when we begin to covet, and God's Word counsels us to be content with what we have (Heb.13:5). But contentment is something that does not come naturally to fallen human nature. It has to be learned (Phil. 4:11-12) and the learning process is provided by the experiences we go through in the good providence of God. When we covet we are resentful that another person has what we do not have but want. We may not need it, but we want it, and sometimes we want it simply because we resent the fact the other person has it. But what God has given the other person may be, without our knowing it, a compensatory blessing for immense battles, struggles and disappointments in his life and service. Even in the area of serving God there can be an element of competition and even envy because our work is not being blessed in the way nor to the extent that some others are experiencing. We need to remember that it is God who works and he uses us in the way that he sees is best. Read the wise prayer in Proverbs 30:7-9 and slay the evil spirit of coveting.

20:18-20

GOD IS NEAR

It is clear that the reaction of the people was to the visible and audible signs of the near presence of God rather than to the content and significance of what God said in the Commandments. They trembled with fear and stayed at a distance (v.18). We are told in Hebrews 12:21 that even Moses trembled with fear, but in today's verses Moses encouraged the people because he saw that their reaction was one of panic. In the previous chapter (Exod. 19:9, 16) we were told about the dramatic circumstances of cloud, thunder and lightning that accompanied God's speaking of the commandments. It is little wonder the people trembled. In such an extraordinary atmosphere there can be such an emotional experience of God's presence that people either do not hear what God is saying or they hear but misunderstand the significance of what is being said. We have an example of this in the story of the Garden of Eden when God, seeking his children, spoke and the sound of his voice caused them immediately to hide from him (Gen. 3:8-10). Of course Adam and Eve had sinned and their guilty consciences constrained them to hide from God rather than to respond to his words, which were words of grace. God was not speaking as the judge of the sinner but rather as the Father of the Prodigal seeking a lost son. No doubt the same reaction is seen here at Sinai. This was a people who had received so much from God, the blessings of salvation, deliverance and life, and yet they had constantly complained and criticised. It was little wonder that they wanted to keep their distance from God. Many people like to think of God 'up there', keeping an eye on things and ready to help in crisis. But to have God come down, to have him come close and have personal dealings in a practical life-governing way is much more alarming. The same reaction was manifested when God came down in his Son, born in Bethlehem (Matt. 2:1-3). In the second giving of the Law in Deuteronomy 5:22-33 Moses reminded the people of the occasion at Sinai, no doubt to make them consider to what extent they really wanted to be with and to deal with God. That is a question we do well to ask ourselves.

A HOLY GOD

The people were truly shaken by the manifestation of the majesty of God and by the fact that this God was speaking to them concerning their whole way of life. Perhaps our generation of evangelical Christians needs to be reminded of the glory of God and the holiness of God so that there might be a recovery of reverence and godly fear in our worship. Think of these words selected from one of F. W. Faber's hymns of worship:

> My God, how wonderful Thou art,
> Thy majesty how bright! ...
> How dread are Thine eternal years,
> O everlasting Lord....
> O how I fear Thee, living God,
> With deepest tenderest fears....
> How beautiful, how beautiful
> The sight of Thee must be,
> Thine endless wisdom, boundless power,
> And awful purity![17]

Think of how Isaiah reacted when he saw the glory of God (Isa. 6:1-5). Of course in today's verses the reaction of the people was the opposite of what God wanted, and perhaps we should see here one of the wiles or stratagems of the Devil seeking to confuse and so to misdirect God's people at a significant stage in their life of service. The people drew back, possibly drawing back from heart commitment, and that is a dangerous attitude which can cost dearly (Heb. 10:22-23, 39). At the same time, in their drawing back, they seemed to recognise that they were in need of a mediator, someone to stand between them and God, someone to act for them and speak for them. It is legitimate to see in this something of a foreshadowing of the great Mediator who is Christ (1 Tim. 2:5). Just as Moses was one of the people, one of themselves, so it was and is with our Lord Jesus Christ. He too is one of us, sharing our life and understanding our needs (Heb. 2:17-18; 4:14-16). Moses' words were full of reassurance. He calmed the fears of the people and pointed out that what God wanted to know was whether or not they were ready to be serious in their faith and obedience.

CHRISTIAN BEHAVIOUR

These verses introduce the section in Exodus dealing with a vast number of rules and regulations regarding the worship and life of God's people. The people were reminded that God had in fact spoken to them from Heaven, not just from a mountain. What God had *said* was to be the basis of all their worship, and not any image or representation of him that they might make according to their own ideas. This is something that must always be remembered. God has spoken. We have his Word, and that Word is the supreme rule of faith and life. It is by the Scriptures that we must direct the faith, worship and life of individual believers and the church. The reference to the altar of earth seems to emphasise the essential simplicity of worship, and when later the altar might be made of stone, it should be unhewn, undecorated stone. It is so easy for fallen human nature to 'decorate' the essential forms of worship, to try to make worship more attractive and thus more acceptable to people. But worship is essentially for God and must be in forms that exalt and honour him. We must always remember in our public worship that if outsiders, enquirers, and those ignorant of Christian things are present, they will get an impression of God from our attitude in what we as believers say and how we behave.

If there is an absence of reverence and an easy-going spirit of 'camaraderie' people may well conclude that God is not to be taken all that seriously. Of course, cold, grim solemnity gives an equally false impression of God. In the last verse of the chapter there is a clear emphasis on modesty of dress lest there be immodesty of behaviour. In Old Testament times ritual nakedness was a feature of many forms of idolatrous worship. In our day seemliness of dress, not just in areas of worship but also in areas of relaxation and pleasure, is something to be taken seriously. It is not enough to claim, 'It does me no harm. It makes me feel better.' Things we do can be a source of temptation to someone else. Jesus said strong words about that (Luke 17:1-2).

21:1-4

GOD'S LABOUR LAWS

This section of Exodus is difficult for us to understand and to apply, because these regulations are set in a culture and a way of life totally different from what we imagine our own to be. The idea of slavery, one person owning another, is abhorrent to us. But in our own society the conditions some work under and the low wages paid to some people, especially domestic helps, is a form of slavery that is indefensible and abhorrent to God. In

Moses' day, slavery seems to have been the general basis of the whole labour system and these regulations govern and restrict the terms of that slavery in order to establish and protect the dignity as well as the rights of the individual. The rights and wrongs of slavery as an institution are not being discussed; nor is slavery being justified; nor is it suggested that we should not work for the abolition of wrongs in society. God's laws or principles of life, developed from the general principles of the Ten Commandments, are to be applied in society as it is, not in some ideal society which might yet come to pass. Note also that we are dealing with Hebrew slaves, indicating that both master and slave are members of the distinctive, redeemed people of God, all of whom had been slaves in Egypt, in circumstances of ruthless totalitarian treatment. Such labour relations were not to be countenanced among God's people. The particular and detailed laws we are now studying are clearly restrictive in their intent, concerned to protect and preserve men and women from harm and humiliation. If we look on to 21:23-24 we see the principle of *only* an eye for an eye, but no excessive revenge. And in 22:27b the God who speaks sternly in the Commandments, and who speaks with great detail concerning a whole range of human relationships and activities, declares himself to be a compassionate Father. We are ready now to look at details.

GOD'S CARE

No master, be it man or woman, is allowed to own another man or woman as a slave (an 'indentured labourer'[18]) in perpetuity. At the end of six years the slave must go free. There seems to be an echo of the 'sabbath' principle in this regulation and it signifies the concern of God for the good and development of human lives. In verse 3 we may assume that the family, as a family, goes free. In verse 4 there seems to be something inhuman unless we see the master, in a real act of kindness, giving the slave one of his own slaves as a wife. The slave's decision not to go free was not simply because he did not want to be separated from his wife and children. It is stated clearly that he loved his master, and he saw that to live as a slave in the context of kindness, fairness, security and fulfilment is better by far than to risk all in a so-called 'free' society. Independence and freedom to live and to express personality according to one's own choice and even inclination sound wonderful concepts. The Prodigal Son thought so, but it did not work out the way he hoped (Luke 15:11-17). He realised after painful experience that he would have been far better off as an obedient son, even with the restrictions of parental rules and family duties. We must also recognise that there are people who, because of various tendencies and limitations of personality and capacity, are not really able to 'stand on their own feet' and who shrink at having to take big decisions. Such people are better off in situations which have real restrictions but which give the security needed for them to be themselves. But note that when the slave said, 'I love my master… I do not want to go free' (a great text for a sermon on dedication), the whole matter was taken to God for expression and confirmation. How we need to take all our decisions to God, particularly decisions about work and relationships. After all, he knows us (Ps. 103:10-14) and he cares about us (1 Pet. 5:7).

21:7-11

RIGHT RELATIONSHIPS

It is fascinating to see that in these long-ago days the laws of God gave greater honour and protection to a woman than to a man. This must be kept in mind so that there is no wrong emotional reaction when we read in the New Testament (1 Pet. 3:7) about giving greater honour to the weaker sex (RSV), partner (NIV), or vessel (AV). The emphasis in today's passage is that the woman, whatever her age, but especially if young and unmarried, must not be made use of, taken advantage of, humiliated or treated as a mere thing or property in order to please and satisfy a man. The idea of a father among the people of God selling a daughter horrifies us, as indeed it did the leader of God's people much later in the story when wrongdoing in social and business life had produced such poverty that fathers were driven to mortgaging and selling their children (Neh. 5:1-9). Perhaps we have to see the situation of the slave-bride in terms of the culture pattern of arranged marriages and dowries, necessary and accepted in order to maintain existence. But, even so, the regulations are clear and strict. The girl had to be treated with respect and value, and if specific things were not done, then she should go totally free. If the man wearied of the relationship, especially if he had made the girl his wife, he might not simply dispose of her. That is regarded as faithlessness before God, something that needs to be remembered by young Christians who have a series of temporary relationships. God is not indifferent to hurt, especially a girl's hurt. The faithless man had to go to the girl's family, to confess his wrong, and to let them redeem or buy her freedom. If the situation was that the man had bought the girl-slave to be his son's wife in due time, then she was virtually his daughter and had to be dealt with and honoured as such. This gives a different slant on slavery. If verse 10 refers to the custom of taking a second wife or a further concubine, the rights of the first wife were jealously guarded, and if the man failed to do right, then the woman would go free. God will take the side of those who are taken advantage of by men who are stronger.

SERIOUS CRIMES

These verses tend to shock a generation that has legally outlawed capital punishment and in fact has sentimental ideas about any kind of punishment. In our day people speak of 'reverence for life', as if this was a new concept, as the great argument against capital punishment. But we have already seen the great extent to which reverence for life and personality are insisted on in God's laws. Deliberate killing, especially of a parent, is such a denial of the value of life and such a deliberate breaking of God's Law in the Ten Commandments that the penalty is radical. In verses 12-13 there is clear distinction between premeditated murder and accidental killing. For what we call 'manslaughter' or 'culpable homicide' there was provision made for safety from family vengeance but not escape from punishment. For deliberate murder there was no escape, even if the murderer took shelter at God's altar. In verse 16 with reference to kidnapping, which then and now could be a very profitable business, the verdict is clear. If the kidnapper was caught with his victim or with the proceeds of his crime he was to be treated as a murderer and would pay the price. No-one was to be allowed to gain in cash or in any other way from crime. There is something exceedingly evil about profiting from 'killing off' another person and God's Law prescribes the ultimate penalty. Present-day laws are much modified in terms of penalty but we must remember that these prescriptions we are studying were for a people under God's gracious discipline at a time when a new stage of God's work of redemption was being established. The issues were long-term and therefore the standards were strict. God was in earnest, and his people had to be of the same mind. The last two verses speak of situations when a fight breaks out, unplanned and with no lethal weapon carried. The injured party recovers and the guilty party must pay compensation for loss of earnings and for medical treatment. That is a thoroughly reasonable and just judgement

21:20-27

TREAT PEOPLE PROPERLY

In these examples of wrongdoing, as in the earlier ones, two things are clear. God sees and knows all about circumstances, intentions and actions. God also makes plain that when wrong has been done it is not enough simply to say sorry. There is the consequence of punishment and there is the need for restitution. Before reacting against verses 20-21 remember that this sets a far higher standard than had prevailed in Moses' day when slaves had no rights at all. The slave may have been the owner's property but, whether a man or a woman, the slave was not a mere thing. Sadistic beating that led to death had to be punished. If the beating was in fact intended strictly as discipline for wrongdoing and had only a temporary effect on the slave, even though very painful, the owner would not be culpable. In verses 22-23 it is not clear why the woman got involved in the brawl between the two men, although it may have been that one was her husband. If there was a miscarriage so that a new but undeveloped life was lost, then compensation had to be paid, but if the woman's life was also lost then the capital sentence was imposed. There is a tremendous emphasis here on the sanctity of life, whether in the womb or in adult form. There is also recognition that a miscarriage is in a very real sense a bereavement, and that interfering with the process of conception and birth is a solemn thing indeed, not to be countenanced lightly. In verse 24 we have the strict limitation of punishment in terms of *only* an eye for an eye. It is so easy when feelings are deeply hurt to give way to ungoverned passion and when that happens the possibility of justice is remote. God's Word does not allow 'tit-for-tat' revenge and, even when we feel that people are getting away with it, we need to remember the words of Romans 12:14-21. Someone has to give an example and set the standard, and if Christian believers do not do so, then who will? Note also at the end of today's passage that the slave-owner's bad-tempered assaults would cost him very dearly. He would lose the slave. God cares about people, and he is not indifferent about the way we treat them.

RESPONSIBILITY

When we do things or fail to do them and others are hurt and damaged, it is so easy to excuse ourselves by saying that we did not know. These verses make plain that accidents and things done in genuine ignorance are pardonable. In 1 Timothy 1:12-16 Paul admits he blasphemed and persecuted the church but says it was in ignorance because of unbelief. After his conversion he knew he had God's forgiveness and yet the sorrow of his wrongdoing remained with him all his life. In verse 28 there is an accident that could happen wherever there are animals, but in verse 29 there is tragedy because of the owner's carelessness and irresponsibility. That owner then had to pay the grim price for a life that was needlessly brought to a premature end. To be careless after having been told, taught and warned is sinful and serious. That is certainly true in moral and spiritual terms for those who have the privilege of sitting under consistent biblical ministry. Such persons cannot ever say they were not told. There is no escape for those who neglect the issue of salvation (Heb. 2:1-3a). It seems from verses 30-32 that in these cases of culpable homicide the death penalty could be avoided by the appropriate 'redemption' and the paying of a 'ransom' price. It is deeply moving that even in such chapters as these our thoughts can be led forward to him who paid the price and died the death so that we could be forgiven (Mark 10:45; 1 Tim. 2:5-6). The price of the slave was thirty shekels of silver but the price paid for our redemption was infinitely greater (1 Pet. 1:18-20). The last verses of our passage again emphasise the sin of carelessness. We are indeed our brother's keeper (Gen. 4:8-10) and we have a responsibility for one another. Christians must learn to bear one another's burdens (Gal. 6:2), to be good Samaritans (Luke 10:29-37), not passing by on the other side saying, 'That's your problem.'

PROTECTION OF PROPERTY

The Israelites were a people not long delivered from oppression and slavery, and history testifies that liberty is not always easy to handle. There has to be law, and the laws must be seen to be reasonable and just, otherwise there will be no confidence in them. When confidence goes chaos results, society becomes confused, standards of honesty disappear and people begin to feel that the wrongdoer is better looked after than the person who seeks to do right. This passage again emphasises restitution for wrongdoing and, as the restitution is greater than the original theft, a significant element of punishment is involved. In verses 2-3 distinction is made between burglary in daylight and at night. Someone breaking through a wall at night could well be a murderer rather than a thief and if the householder acts radically in his own defence in the dark he is not held guilty. But if it is daylight, he can see what is going on and can recognise the wrongdoer and must not take the law into his own hands in terms of execution. In verse 5 restitution has to be of the best quality. There must be no cheap compensation. It must be 'new for old' as many insurance companies provide in our own day. Careless or deliberate fire-raising costs the guilty person full restitution. Right through this passage there is balance and reasonableness, but there is also a recognition that human nature is not always to be trusted and that people, even God's redeemed people, do in fact at times deal wrongly with each other. Read carefully verses 7-11 and see how all uncertain issues involving honesty and reputation have to be brought to God for the truth to be made plain. How God made things plain is not stated, but there is an indication in verse 11 that a person's oath or word before God was taken as truth. Note also in verse 9 that the idea that 'finders are keepers', is not allowed. If you keep what belongs to another, it is stealing, and that is forbidden in the Commandments. The details of passages such as this make plain that the whole of life and activity is to be governed by God's standards. When people accept this principle and act on it, then society is healthy.

22:16-17

SEXUAL BEHAVIOUR

These are searching and shattering words for a generation like ours in which sexual activity outside marriage is taken by many as the norm and regarded as acceptable. Even from early teenage years promiscuity is considered so commonplace that the only concern seems to be to limit the consequences of pregnancy or disease. Note first that this subject follows on from the first half of the chapter that dealt with various forms of stealing. The reference may be to the fact that the unmarried daughter was thought of as the property of the father and she, having been violated, would no longer bring to her father the expected marriage dowry. But the stern nature of the words used and the regulation prescribed suggest rather that the man was stealing from the girl what he had no right to steal, namely her virginity and purity. Having done this, the man was reckoned to be married to the girl: he must pay the appropriate dowry, and formally and officially marry her. The man no longer had any rights in the situation. It belonged to the girl's father to decide whether or not marriage would be suitable in the circumstances and if his approval was not given, the man who sinned against the girl still had to pay the marriage dowry. He had done wrong and he had to be punished. Relationships and behaviour in them are matters of great concern to God. The current attitude to sexual relationships outside marriage and to all sexual promiscuity flies in the face of God's declared standards. God says immorality is wrong, and sex must be kept for marriage, where it will be a true expression and fulfilment of human love. That there are serious consequences from sexual sin is clear from Ephesians 5:3-6. That there is forgiveness for the penitent is clear from John 8:1-11. These issues are very important.

THE OCCULT

Sorcery, bestiality and idolatry were common features of the life of the nations among which Israel had to live and witness to God. God's Law speaks with categorical prohibition on all three matters. God's people then and now are called to be different and distinct in behaviour as well as belief. Even though the penalty of death for these wrongs does not seem to have been operative in New Testament times the fact of God's abhorrence of them is stated beyond doubt (1 Cor. 6:9-11). Whether we speak of magic, sorcery, witchcraft, spiritism, the occult, or use any other descriptive name, the message is plain. There must be no trafficking of any kind with evil spirits, whether it is in trying to know the future or control it – our own or that of other people. When there are things we neither know nor understand, the thing to do is to have faith in God who can be trusted utterly. To turn to other sources for comfort, whether in the realm of 'ouija boards' or in the so-called fun of 'fortune telling', is both unwise and dangerous because, as many have found out to their cost, no-one can control evil spirits apart from Jesus. The man who tried it in Acts 19:11-20 got the fright of his life. Read the explicit prohibition in Deuteronomy 18:9-14. Read also Acts 13:6-10; 19:19; 1 Corinthians 10:18-22; Isaiah 8:19. (There is a full and detailed article on 'Magic and Sorcery' in *The Illustrated Bible Dictionary*[19]). One of the many references given is Ezekiel 13:17-23 where the practitioners of evil were women, and reference is made to magic bands and such things used as 'charms'. The subtle and seemingly innocent start of becoming involved with 'luck' rather than trusting God is seen when even Christians can be heard saying, 'touch wood'. We need to remember that there is a world of spirits who are contrary to God (1 John 5:19; Eph. 6:10-12). But we must also remember that Jesus Christ has conquered the whole kingdom of principalities and powers in order to set us free (Col.2:13-15). To trifle with the occult in any form is to risk being entangled to our destruction.

22:18-20

SIN JUDGED; SINNERS FORGIVEN

The reference to bestiality (v.19) will shock and horrify some but, as evil comes more and more out into the open in our day and generation, we are compelled to see to what extent godless human nature can degenerate, not just to indulgence but to depravity and to what is unnatural. Bestiality, which featured in some pagan rituals, was a capital crime in Israel as was homosexual practice (Lev. 20:13-16; Rom. 1:24-32). No-one likes to read and think about these things and circumstances have sheltered many from any contact with the cruder manifestations of these ugly things. Of course, newspapers, magazines and television are forcing these subjects into our consciousness. Some have to help pastorally those who are crushed with guilt and scarred in personality because of sins in sexual realms. Some have been more sinned against than sinning. Some were trapped and manipulated by evil men and women in their youth and the scars have affected them in a costly way all through their lives. We read in the Press of some evildoers being brought to judgement years after their crimes but we need to remember that there is another Day of Judgement when all evildoers will stand before God and the books of record will be opened. God knows everything! Some in deepest penitence cry out for forgiveness, cleansing and deliverance. Never forget that Jesus Christ came into the world to save sinners (1 Tim. 1:15), to break the power of cancelled sin, and to re-channel human potential into areas of safety, certainty, enjoyment, and Christian service. Read the glorious affirmation in 1 Corinthians 6:9-11: 'Such were some of you, but you were washed.' Read the wise counsel of Galatians 6:1-3. Christians are in the business of salvation and restoration, not judgement and demolition. But some things are wrong and must be declared to be wrong and God pronounces his judgement on them. Note the reference in verse 20 to idolatry, making a god to suit our own imaginings and desiring. To do that is to reject God out of hand.

SHOWING CARE

These verses deal with the underprivileged and show clearly that God is not dealing only with the ugly manifestations of fallen human nature. Of course, the neglect of others stems from selfishness, which is simply self-centredness and that can be very ugly and cruel at times. We can wrong the strangers by ignoring them, even when they sit near us in church. We can oppress the stranger, who may actually be a regular attender at church, by being so deliberately preoccupied with our own little circle of friends that we forget all about him or her. There are those in most congregations who feel 'left out' and are given the impression that they don't belong and are not wanted. This is a denial of the grace of God and we need to remember that when we were far off, strangers to grace and to God, God came to us and drew us in with the generous welcome of redeeming love (Eph. 2:11-13, 19). The widow and orphan may get a lot of attention at the immediate time of bereavement and loss, but the isolation and loneliness can later on envelop them. If the widow is being treated unjustly, who speaks up for her? God says he will do so (Ps. 68:5) and he is angry when we fail to do so. Consider the description of pure religion in James 1:27. When did we actually visit a widow, widower, orphan or lonely single person? We may have prayed for them. But have we visited them? Read Deuteronomy 24:19-21. What a care God has, and he insists that we too should have a care for the needy. We may feel that *we* are the needy ones longing for care and kindness, and that may well be true. But do we always think about ourselves rather than others? In the area of care it is very often in giving that we get. Read Proverbs 11:24. Of course love given is not always responded to. Really to love lays you open to hurt. God knows how true that is and his hurt is expressed in passages such as Isaiah 1:2-3. Ultimately his love was expressed in human flesh and blood terms. The Word was made flesh and dwelt among us (John 1:14; Heb. 1:1-2). That is why a prayer without a visit or a conversation can be less than Christian.

22:25-27

MONEY MATTERS

Lending money to a fellow believer or to a friend can complicate the relationship in various ways. The feeling of being in debt, even to a friend, can induce a sense of guilt, or failure, or even jealousy and resentment. If, as is often the case with money-lenders, the rate of interest is very high, the borrower becomes trapped in a spiral of debt that eventually demoralises and destroys. Even an interest-free loan has to be handled carefully on both sides. Here an Israelite is forbidden to charge interest from another Israelite. In this way a loan becomes a practical help, a genuinely gracious act, rather than a means of profit. Only those who have known really straitened circumstances can understand the painful feeling of shame and hurt involved in going to ask for a loan, especially from someone who knows you well. Many would rather go without help. Perhaps all of us who have been well provided for by God in his goodness should be more aware of the needs and circumstances of those who may be living on the borderline of poverty. But even then, the manner in which we seek to help must be such that the human dignity of the one in need is not breached. A little thought and care nurtured by genuine prayer will soon discover opportunities to help in such a way that all the praise and thanksgiving will be given to God. In verse 26 it seems to be permissible to take some pledge from the neighbour as a guarantee that the loan would be repaid, though it would be a heartless person who did that. It would be tantamount to saying that you did not really trust the one being given the loan. In any case, the poor person might have as his only worthwhile possession the 'garment' or 'cloak' or 'poncho' a shepherd would wear and which would serve as a blanket at night. God insisted that the cloak be returned at night time, no doubt pledged again in the morning, and becoming a daily reminder of the humiliation of having had to borrow. If the poor man cried, God would hear, because he is compassionate. That is the standard of care. That is the kind of God we have.

_22:28-31_

RESPECT FOR AUTHORITY

Two very different things seem to be brought together in verse 28. The third Commandment makes it perfectly clear that we must not blaspheme or curse God. This stands as a constant rebuke to many in our generation, even in high places, who use the name of God and of Jesus Christ his Son in such a casual, devaluing, blasphemous way. But the prohibition may well apply to casual attitudes in worship, when we profess to be dealing with God. We must let God be God and, to say the least, treat him and speak to him with the respect that is due to his name. The instruction not to revile a ruler is not easily followed in our day when so many in authority live personal lives that do not invite respect or trust. Of course this is nothing new as the story of Herod makes plain (Mark 6:14-28). It is a fact that some officers of authority have shown themselves to be false and untrustworthy, using their power wrongly. But in Acts 23:1-5 we find Paul quoting Exodus 22:28 even when the High Priest acted in a way totally out of order. Resentment at authority, secular or spiritual, can so easily become a spirit of lawlessness which leads to all manner of evil. We are taught in the New Testament to pray for those who are in places of authority (Rom. 13:1-7; 1Tim. 2:1-4). We are also taught the principle of mutual submission in Ephesians 5:21 and 1 Peter 5:5-6. This is something that 'goes against the grain' of assertive human nature. The chapter ends with the insistence that the governing principle which keeps the whole of life on a healthy course is to see to it that God is given what is his rightful due. It is as we are dealing rightly with God that we become able and desirous of dealing properly with people. We need to remember that all we are and all we have is the gift of God's grace (1 Cor. 4:7). We are not our own but, bought with a price, we belong to God. Our whole way of life should testify to that in a recognisable way (1 Cor. 6:18-20).

LISTEN TO GOD

These verses continue to apply the principles of the Ten Commandments to actual situations in the life of society and the demand here is for absolute integrity in matters of justice. There must be no false witness, no collusion among witnesses, no favouritism simply because a man is poor and no prejudice simply because a man is an enemy. If an enemy's beast has strayed you must take it back to him, and if an enemy is injured in an accident you must rescue and help him. If a man is poor and unable to press his own case you must not take advantage of his weakness. Any suggestion of a bribe, whatever the 'currency', must be refused, because it would have the effect of blinding you to the justice of the case. These counsels which apply to official court cases also apply to the area of relationships and gossip. Uttering a false report (v.1) can apply to passing on bits of information you may have heard even though you may not be sure of their truth. The false charge (v.7) can apply to the hints made about someone's character. Even though they are proved to be untrue some of the 'mud' sticks and a person can be under unjust suspicion or even ostracism for a long time. God declares that he will deal with the perpetrators of such false charges. In verses 4-5 we see that 'loving our enemies' has to do with actions and attitudes rather than feelings, but often when we do the right thing the appropriate feelings begin to come, or at least the wrong feelings begin to subside. There is wise and kind counsel in verse 9. God reminded the Israelites that they knew full well what it was like to be the stranger, unsure, hesitant, afraid of the unknown, and aware of the antagonism that could so easily become persecution. One last comment needs to be made on verse 2a. Don't follow the crowd. Don't be deceived by the words, 'Everybody does it.' That is usually a lie and, even if most people do something, the majority and public opinion are not always right. Learn to listen to God and, when persuaded, stand your ground even if you stand alone.

23:10-19

LEARN TO STOP

I n chapters 21-23 we see many examples of God's concern for justice and his wonderful care for his people, for those having a struggle, and for the whole of his creation. There is an emphasis on conservation in verses 10-11. The principle of Sabbath rest is applied to the use of the land and the benefits go to the poor and to the animals. The Sabbath, as God instituted it at the time of creation (Gen. 2:1-3), is given to man as a means of blessing, not as an irksome restriction. It is an indication of how far man has excluded God from his thinking that both public demand and government legislation for destroying the Sabbath have been so prominent in our day. If the ground can become exhausted and unproductive when it does not have its rightful rest, it is certainly true that men and women who go on and on without the pattern of a day of rest will soon decline in energy and capacity. Our generation has had to invent the term 'burn-out' because so many are jaded and spent long before middle-age, let alone old age. Too many ministers and Christian workers are on the treadmill of ceaseless work; too many Christians are involved in too many Christian activities, with no other interests, no non-Christian friends and no time to think. Some, of course, have too many hobbies and interests. Either way the hours of each day are committed and mortgaged for weeks and even months ahead, to such an extent that if God called for a specific service of some urgency it would not be possible to fit him in. We all need to learn to stop, not least to have time to think and to pray. We all need to learn at times to leave good things undone, and to do so without feeling guilty. If we fail to learn, then we are rulers and directors of our own lives; we are conforming to the business pattern and dictates of this mad age; we are serving other gods.

SPIRITUAL WORSHIP

The verses dealing with the application of the Sabbath principle lead right on to the theme of worship. One of the great blessings of the Sabbath is the opportunity to draw near to God without distraction: in worship, thanksgiving, remembrance, prayer, and to hear his Word. God wants his people's love and fellowship, not just obedience to his laws. The people were to observe the Feast of Unleavened Bread, which is the Passover, and so to remember the great thing God did for them in saving them out of the land of Egypt (Exod. 12:14-20). We do the same when we gather at the Lord's Table to remember the body that was broken and the blood that was shed for our salvation. The Feast of Harvest (or Firstfruits or Weeks, v.16a), took place seven weeks after Passover (Deut. 16:9-12), and this corresponds to Pentecost, fifty days after Easter Monday. The Feast of Ingathering refers to the final harvest of the year, sometimes referred to as the Feast of Tabernacles and, while there may be some reference to remembering Israel's pilgrim journeys, the main emphasis seems to be that of rejoicing in the completion of the labour of the whole year. Note that in Deuteronomy 16:1-17, where the three feasts are spoken of, the Passover is regarded as the beginning of the harvest; the gathered grain speaks of provision for all their needs; and the harvest is the final rejoicing. The Passover looks back to the victory of the death of the Lamb of God. The Feast of Weeks or Pentecost speaks of God's full provision for life and service by the Holy Spirit who has been given to us. The final harvest speaks of the fulfilment of all God's plan of salvation in the coming of the Kingdom. The past is dealt with. The present is provided for. The future is sure and guaranteed. Paul speaks of this in terms of peace, grace and glory in Romans 5:1-5.

23:20-22

THE GOD WHO LEADS

God now directed the thoughts of his people to the way that lay ahead of them. They were to recognise clearly that theirs was not a mere human venture, but a spiritual programme directed from Heaven by an angel. This 'angel' could refer to a God-appointed leader such as Moses or Joshua or to a supernatural messenger, an angel in the generally accepted sense. Whether this angel would be visible or not is not stated. The pillars of cloud and of fire (Exod. 13:21-22), symbols of God's presence, were certainly visible. The emphasis in verse 20 is on God's provision and it is full of encouragement and assurance. This angel messenger, who carried the authority of God, would go before them in their journey. Think of the Risen Christ in Matthew 28:7 who promises to go before his disciples. The angel not only marks out the route, he guards and protects the people and the work, and brings both to the God-appointed place that is prepared for them. We must apply these promises, and the similar one in John 14:2, to the ongoing business of life and service here and now in this world. We must not postpone the 'place prepared' to Heaven. Think of God's wonderful promise to Jacob in Genesis 28:15. The thought of being led in life's journey is a comforting one indeed. We *are led*; we do not lead! And we are led by the angel of God's presence (Isa. 63:9), full of care, compassion and understanding. But there is a serious side to all this. Whether the angel signifies God's personal presence or his personal representative, human or divine, there must be obedience. God's name is in the angel, and to disobey the angel is to go against God. This is not a light thing. There are consequences: 'he will not pardon your transgressions' (AV), because disobedience hinders and harms the work of God and gives opportunity to the enemy. There will always be enemies, because the people of God move forward to take possession of territory held by the powers and persons of evil who will resist with all their might. But when we go forward in the obedience of faith, our God fights for us. He takes it personally when hands and voices are raised against us.

EVIL IS REAL

T he grim emphasis of these verses is understandable when once we recognise the real, destructive, anti-God and anti-human-life nature of evil. Human sin works all kinds of evil, to harrow life and experience (Jas 1:13-15), and there is evil that goes beyond mere human badness and becomes demonic. When devilish evil becomes established and manifests itself in the form of kingdoms, philosophies and attitudes that are determined in their collaboration to oppose all that is of God, there simply cannot be neutrality. The nations and peoples listed in verse 23 had sold themselves to evil. They had made their choice and would not move from it. Their judgement was necessary not only because they were evil in themselves but because, if they were allowed to remain and operate, they would poison, corrupt and seduce God's people and lead them away into catastrophe. The Israelites were told not to tamper with or compromise with evil, even when it had a religious appearance in attractive monuments (v.24). We need to remember that there are areas and activities in society today that are positive dangers to spiritual life and these can so debilitate Christian life that Christian service simply shrivels. The future experience of the Israelites was to be warfare and they were to be led into it by

God's presence. There was also the promise that God would prepare for them a table of blessing in the presence of their enemies (Ps. 23:5). It is a fact that many have proved their richest, deepest and sweetest blessings have been found right at the heart of spiritual battle. It is still a solemn thought that God's people, who are by no means free from flaws and faults, are used by God as instruments of judgement as well as instruments of salvation (2 Cor. 2:15-16). But if we look back to Genesis 15:16 we see that for generations the iniquity of the Amorites and their allies had been building up to the point when judgement was inevitable.

23:23-33

GOD'S WAYS ARE RIGHT

God's methodology is stated clearly in verses 29-30. He knows what he is doing and knows the most effective way of doing it. Right through the passage there is repeated emphasis on the words, 'I will'. It is God who is working, and we always need to be quite clear that without him and apart from him we can do nothing (John 15:5). There is neither question of, nor limitation of, God's absolute sovereignty and power, and without doubt he could sweep away every manifestation of evil in an instant (Ps. 2:1-6; 2 Thes. 2:7-8). But God chooses and ordains to work little by little (v.30), and that for good reasons. If the evil nations were swept away in one massive clearance, there would be territory left unoccupied, uncultivated, with no-one yet able to take over the administration. That would result in a reversion to jungle conditions which would be of no benefit and would leave a legacy of additional clearing up. Situations and lives left in a state of emptiness lead to the last state being worse than the first, as Jesus made plain in Matthew 12:43-45. Whether in individual or congregational life, simply to stop things because they are secular and in no way specifically Christian and do not seem to contribute anything positive in relation to the gospel, may not be the right way to act in the first instance. Granted there are situations when immediate action is necessary. But we need discernment, and that is learned through experience. An untaught congregation will not necessarily understand why certain things are done and if they are perplexed they may well resent and react. The principle God enunciates here is one of gradual and progressive supplanting or replacing. It is made plain in verse 30 that it was only as the people were 'increased', that is, when they had grown in spiritual stature and capacity and not just in numbers, that they would be able to possess the land. Possessing means much more than just being there. It calls for people who are spiritually able to administer rightly what belongs to

God. Easy victories and easy advances lead to spiritual lassitude and complacency, not to spiritual maturity.

GOD'S PROVISION

Look back to Exodus 23:31 where the boundaries of the territory promised to the Israelites are described. It is doubtful if this vast area was ever fully occupied by the Israelites even in the great days of David and Solomon and we need not consider this promise simply in territorial terms. It must have been staggering to this people, so recently delivered from slavery in Egypt, to think that such extensive blessing could ever be theirs. The possibilities were limitless. In like manner *we* often fail to grasp the extent and possibilities of the blessings that are promised us in Christ. God has blessed us with every spiritual blessing (Eph. 1:3); He has given us all things necessary for life and for godliness (2 Pet. 1:3-11), and all has been given us in rich measure to enjoy (1 Tim. 6:17). No eye has seen, no ear has heard, no mind has conceived what God has prepared for those who love him (1 Cor. 2:9). This is God's provision. But note that while God said he would deliver the situation into the hands of his people, they were the ones who would do the driving out. These verses flow right on from Exodus

23:31-33 and take up the historical narrative from where it left off in 20:21. The section we have studied from 20:22 to 23:33 has contained the 'case-law' based on the Ten Commandments. The basic principles having been stated in the Commandments and the detailed applications having been declared, the whole 'covenant' now had to be ratified or agreed to by the people. Four men were named by God, together with seventy others to represent all the people, and they were to ascend the mountain while the generality of the people remained below at a distance, as they had chosen (20:18-20). Moses alone was to come near to God, the other three men seemingly remaining at a little distance. It reminds us of Jesus alone in Gethsemane with his three friends nearby. It was a tremendous occasion for the three men with Moses, but it seems to have made the sons of Aaron spiritually proud and arrogant. The story is in Leviticus 10:1-3 and Numbers 3:1-4. It needs a humble heart to keep ourselves usable when God blesses.

24:3-8

GOD'S COVENANT

S uch is the coming and going in relation to God's presence on the mountain that it is difficult to keep the sequence clear. These verses seem to follow on from Exodus 20:21

when Moses returned to the people after his solitary audience with God. If this is so, then we can imagine something of the high pitch of emotional excitement among the people. Moses told them all the details of the covenant, and without hesitation the people agreed. Whether they did this with understanding and with genuine commitment of heart and life, or whether it was done because the occasion demanded such a public act of commitment, or whether it was out of fear lest God be angry, we cannot really tell. Public acts of dedication, especially when large numbers are involved, are difficult to evaluate. Time will reveal to what extent there will be the obedience of faith. All the words from God were then written in a book (v.4), not least to preserve the exact terms in which God had spoken. Oral tradition is notoriously inaccurate and liable to distortion and this is why we have the Scriptures given by the sovereign inspiration of the Holy Spirit (2 Tim. 3:16). In the morning an altar was built, sacrifices were arranged, the written covenant was read again, and again all the people gave their assent. But no matter how willing people were to enter into a covenant or relationship or fellowship with God, as his people, it could not be without the shedding of the blood of the sacrifice that speaks of atonement made for sin. The covenant was sealed with blood. Did the people remember the night of the Passover? The plan and the pattern of salvation were from God. Think of the hymn often sung at the Lord's Table:

> 'My blood I thus pour forth,' He cries,
> 'To cleanse the soul in sin that lies;
> In this the covenant is sealed,
> And Heaven's eternal grace revealed.'[20]

24:9-11

GOD IS LIGHT

This whole chapter seems to be full of contrasts and even contradictions. In verse 2 only Moses was invited to come near and yet in these verses we are told that all 74 men went up, saw the God of Israel, and shared together in a feast of worship and communion. Nadab and Abihu, who were later to prove false, were there and it makes us think of how Judas Iscariot sat at table with Jesus and the disciples in the upper room (Matt. 26:17-30). In the bright shining presence of God, and seeing his glory, there seems to have been no sense of fear, although there was certainly a spirit of reverence and worship, indicated by the reference to the clearness and purity under the feet of God. We sing sometimes, 'How beautiful, how beautiful, the sight of Thee must be',[21] and at the Lord's Table we sometimes sing, 'Here, O my Lord, I see Thee face to face'.[22] In another hymn we sing, 'Immortal, invisible, God only wise, in light inaccessible hid from our eyes', and that hymn goes on to say that it is the splendour of light that hides God from our eyes.[23] We are told in 2 Corinthians 4:6 that we see the glory of God in the face of Jesus Christ, because he is the exact representation of God (Heb. 1:3; John 1:14; 2 Pet. 1:16). Earlier in the narrative the people were aware of God in terms of thunder and lightning (Exod. 20:18), but now the glory of God is spoken of in terms of surpassing beauty, gentleness and peace. The meaning of the reference to God not laying his hand on the chief men, who were representatives of the people, seems to be that being so near to God did not harm them in any way. Of course, it was on the basis of a sacrifice that atoned for sin that they were acceptable in God's presence and so richly blessed. God's glory and his goodness are inseparable, as Exodus 33:18-23 makes plain. Having read this passage, think of 'the Lamb's great bridal feast of bliss and love'.[24] We have a God who can be loved and trusted. There are indeed no shadows at all with him (Jas 1:17).

THE NEAR PRESENCE OF GOD

God again called Moses into his near presence, with the specific purpose of receiving the two tablets of stone with the Ten Commandments inscribed on them by the finger of God, an indication of both the authority and permanence of these laws. Knowing that he would be absent for some time, Moses left Aaron and Hur, men of prayer, to watch over and to guide the people. It is not clear whether God commanded Moses to take with him Joshua, his servant or minister. But in view of the fact that Joshua, having already proved himself in battle (Exod. 17:8-10), was later to take over the leadership of the people, this experience would be part of his preparation. Joshua would see clearly how God dealt with Moses and that would mean a great deal when in due time God spoke the great words of encouragement in Joshua 1:1-9. The cloud and the glory that settled on Mount Sinai both signify the presence of God. For six days Moses dwelt at the summit of the mountain and not until the seventh day, when God spoke specifically, did Moses enter into the cloud. The Psalmist speaks of the blessedness of the man who is called to approach God's presence (Ps. 65:4) but also speaks of the kind of man who dares to ascend the hill of God (Ps. 24:3-4). For the people down below the scene was awesome, like devouring fire. They knew their God-given leader was there. They knew they had vowed to obey their God and Moses had been a witness to it. It was all so humanly impressive that we feel the people should have been drawn to an ever deeper commitment to God and to a new spirit of worship. They were spiritually impressed, but as the 40 days went past the impression faded. The influence of the man of God was not personally present. They were at a significant crisis point in spiritual life and service. But, as 32:1, 7-8 will make plain, their spirituality was very shallow.

25:1-9

FROM THE HEART

At this point there is a break in the narrative concerning the experiences of the Israelites and we do not return to the history until chapters 32 and 33. In chapters 25-31 and chapters 34-40 we are given details of the Tabernacle, the place of Israel's worship, which was to be carried with them as they journeyed on. Fourteen chapters are given to instruct us regarding worship. (In Genesis only three chapters deal with the creation of the world, the Garden of Eden and the Fall of man.) Some may be apprehensive about daily study of such detail. But the Old Testament Scriptures constantly point to Jesus, his saving death and glorious resurrection and if we fail to see this then we are like the slow-to-believe disciples on the road to Emmaus (Luke 24:25-27, 44-48). One lesson in particular is clear. If we are to worship God we must do so in the way he has revealed and on the basis he has provided. Worship is much more than a happy time singing hymns. It is more important that God should be honoured than that we should enjoy what we have decided to do. And, underlying all worship and directing it, there is the Word God has spoken. All the materials for the Tabernacle were to be provided by the freewill offerings of the people. There was no compulsion because only that which is given from a willing heart, whether money or service, is worthy of God and a pleasure to him (2 Cor. 8:1-5; 9:7). A tremendous amount of material of great value was needed for setting up the Tabernacle and at first it may seem strange that a people so recently delivered from slavery should have such wealth. But God the great provider had planned in advance and the riches needed for God's work had been pressed on the Israelites by the Egyptians at the time of the Exodus (Exod. 12:33-36). Those who gave willingly simply recognised that all they had was given by God and therefore held in trust by them for God's work. Of course, when *we* think of the price that was paid for our salvation (1 Pet. 1:18-19), there should be a willing and sacrificial spirit in all of us. This makes the uplifting and dedication of the offering in a church service an integral part of worship. It was as the Israelites forgot both God and his Word that they went adrift so soon (Exod. 32). They forgot that they were God's people whom he had redeemed. All they were, their existence as a people, their present life and blessing, and their future hopes and possibilities were all theirs by the grace of God and by his grace alone. It is when we forget all we owe and what we are for that we begin to go astray. It is grateful hearts that offer gladly to God. This is spiritual worship.

25:1-9

ONLY THE BEST

God had saved and delivered his people from their bondage in the land of Egypt and was leading them into the future planned for them. God had given his people his Law in the Ten Commandments which declared his standards and demands, and which stood to condemn them. It is by the Law of God that there comes the knowledge of sin (Rom. 3:19-20) and with that knowledge comes the consciousness of the need for a Saviour. But God has no desire to be remote from his people, whom he has loved with an everlasting love (Jer. 31:3), and he desires to dwell in the midst of them (v.8). But how can men and women defiled by sin enter into fellowship with a holy God, and live happily in his presence? The Tabernacle, in all its astonishing detail which points to Christ in so many ways, gives us a picture of how we come to God in worship; how we have fellowship with him; and on what basis we serve him. Everything about the Tabernacle had to be done in accordance with God's detailed instruction, which he would reveal to and through Moses (v.9). There was to be no place for the 'bright ideas' and 'novel suggestions' which might come from people seeking to make their impact on the worship of God's people. Nowadays there is a vast range of places, other than in church, where men and women can exercise and display their various gifts and inventiveness, finding fulfilment in the process and often expressing spiritual truths. But if 'self' in any form intrudes upon God's dwelling place, the focus will be on people, not on Christ. In 1 Corinthians 1:17 Paul speaks of how human cleverness can make the Cross of no effect and in 2 Corinthians 4:2-5 (AV) emphasises that a wrong spirit in our hearts can hide the gospel from those who need it. All of God's worship and work must be done in God's way and in accordance with God's Word.

THE MEANING OF THE TABERNACLE

I n order to understand these chapters we need to try to visualise the Tabernacle. It was to be made up of three sections set within each other, on the same principle as a castle, with the most important area protected by a series of walls. The only entrance was through the outer court. Within this courtyard there was 'the holy place' and at the back of this a curtain screened off the holiest place of all. In the innermost shrine there stood the Ark, a wooden chest overlaid with gold both inside and out. Note carefully that the description of the Tabernacle begins at the heart, the 'Mercy Seat' (v.17 AV) or the atonement cover. In the Ark there was to be placed the Testimony, the two Tables of the Commandments, the witness that God had spoken and that his Word still speaks. It was to be at the Mercy Seat that God would meet with his people and speak to them and with them, and it is at the Mercy Seat that we can speak with God. The Ark of the Covenant (as it is often referred to) signified God's commitment to his people. The Mercy Seat speaks of atonement for sin and God's own presence. The Tabernacle as a whole portrays the salvation of God which is in Jesus Christ by his atoning death. It is possible to see pointers to Christ in the many different materials specified. Some suggest the gold symbolises the divinity of Christ and the silver the Redeemer; the rich coloured materials point to his kingship and majesty; the dark goats' hair the solemn sin-bearer; the fine linen the purity of Christ's human character; and the oil for the lamps could well speak of the Holy Spirit. We must not get lost in the mass of detail, but concentrate rather on the main aspects of the Tabernacle, remembering that the details of how it all fitted together speak to us of the perfection, in every way, of the salvation that God has accomplished for his people.

25:10-22

GOD'S DWELLING PLACE

The Epistle to the Hebrews helps us to understand the significance of the Tabernacle. Hebrews 4:14-16 speaks of drawing near to God and seems to link the Throne of Grace with the Mercy Seat, and in Hebrews 9:1-14 the pattern of the Tabernacle is specifically spoken of as fore-shadowing Christ's mighty work of salvation. In Hebrews 10:19-25 we have familiar words that encourage us to draw near to God at that Mercy Seat, in the assurance of acceptance and blessing. These are the spiritual messages that were communicated to the Israelites by the symbolism of the Tabernacle. In the same way the symbols in the Communion Service, although remaining only bread and wine, speak to us of the saving death of our Saviour. The two cherubim may signify the over-arching, sovereign protection exercised by God himself in respect of all that he has revealed of himself and his great salvation. When the Israelites were on their journeys the Ark was carried before them (Num. 10:33-36) as a symbol of God's presence, guidance and protection. No human hand was to touch it: an emphasis on the holiness of God and the need for deepest reverence with regard to everything pertaining to God. Read again verse 22 and think how the Israelites, remembering what had been said, would know and feel, 'God with us'. Take time to ponder and to be thrilled by God's clearly stated desire to live in close fellowship with his people (v.8). Think of Jesus' words in John 14:23. It is almost beyond our capacity to grasp the astonishing fact that the Father and the Son by the Holy Spirit desire to be at home with us.

25:23-30

GOD'S BREAD

oving out from the heart of the Tabernacle, the Most Holy Place, the place 'where God dwells', we are told next about articles to be placed in the

inner courtyard, the holy place. The first to be described is the table on which was displayed the Bread of the Presence. The table was portable, as all the parts of the Tabernacle had to be when a people were constantly on their journeys. The similarity in the description of the Table and the Ark indicates that they both speak of Christ. Jesus spoke of the bread of God come down from Heaven and declared himself to be the Bread of Life. The bread of the Presence may emphasise again the presence of God with and for his people to meet their need, and it may also signify bread presented before God as a constant reminder of and thanksgiving for his past mercies. The bread was laid on the table each Sabbath (Lev. 24:5-9). If it was eaten by the priests after seven days there is a suggestion that it miraculously remained fresh. If, as some suggest, it was actually renewed daily then there may be an indication that it was in some way a reminder of the manna in the wilderness and there may be a hint of this in the words about daily bread in the Lord's Prayer. Of course, as Jesus said in reply to the Devil's temptation, 'Man shall not live on bread alone, but on every word that comes from the mouth of God' (Matt. 4:4; Deut. 8:2-3). Jesus is God's Word (John 1:1-2, 14), his full and final word (Heb.1:1-3) and that Word is the bread of our souls by which we live and grow. The Bread of the Presence should make us ponder, receive and rejoice in Jesus' words in John 6:25-35, 48-58.

GOD'S LIGHT

The next feature of the inner court is the lamp-stand. It was to be made of pure gold, not acacia wood covered with gold, and was to be all of one piece. The details are so complex that it is difficult to be sure of its exact appearance. Those of an artistic temperament may try to visualise the cups shaped like almond flowers, and the other items of beauty, but we must not lose sight of the main picture by concentrating on detail. The general opinion is of a central stem with three branches curving up from each side giving seven 'lights' all on one level. It is one candlestick giving one light in sevenfold unity and perfection. Its purpose is stated simply in verse 37 and we think at once of Jesus as the light of the world (John 8:12). The gold was pure, symbolising the purity of Christ, without spot or blemish (1 Pet. 1:19), and the gold was hammered out, suggesting thoughts of how Christ was 'made perfect' through suffering (Heb. 2:10). We do well to ponder how in our own Christian lives the disciplines of the fire and hammer of daily experience mould and fashion us to be useful instruments in the service of the gospel. Jesus is the Light of the world but he also said that we are the light of the world and must shine in the darkness (Matt. 5:14-16). Paul summons us to shine as lights in a dark and perverse generation (Phil. 2:15-16). Of course the only way to do this is to walk in the light (1 John 1:5-7), out in the open with God, seeing to it that our lives are such that they serve as windows or reflectors for the light to shine clearly. In a sense we are the lamp-stand to hold up the Light of the World so that the world around us might see light. Remember, of course, that light and dark always fight.

25:31-40

GOD'S OIL

There is no actual mention here of oil for the lamps, although it was listed in verse 6, but without oil the lamp-stand would be only a piece of furniture, perhaps to be admired, but of no practical use in the business of giving light. Other passages help us to grasp more fully the 'message' of the seven-branched candlestick. In Zechariah 4:1-6 the picture of the lamp does not correspond in detail to the one in the Tabernacle but the prophet is expected to recognise it as such. The empowering oil for the lamp comes in endless and unlimited supply from the olive tree. In Scripture oil is very often a symbol of the Holy Spirit, and just as God's love is poured out into our hearts by the Holy Spirit (Rom. 5:5) so the enabling power of the Holy Spirit is given to us for life and service. The prayer, 'Give me oil in my lamp, keep me burning', is a valid and biblical one but the emphasis is not on *our* having the oil but on the light it enables us to provide. In the lamp-stand the oil was contained in cups or shallow bowls with the burning wick either fixed or floating in it. The wick in itself was nothing and without oil would simply smoke and char, but with the oil there would be clear light, provided the wick was kept trimmed (and that takes watchfulness and careful attention). The lessons for careful Christian living are clear. Never forget Jesus' words, 'Apart from me you can do nothing' (John 15:5). That will keep us from pride when we are too aware of the fact that God is using us in his service. The final passages to glance at are Revelation 1:12-20. Again the sevenfold perfection is emphasised, and the details differ, but the emphasis is on light. The lamp-stands in the hand of Christ are spoken of as the churches, with Christ in the midst. In Revelation 3:20 Christ as the light of the world is portrayed as being outside the church desiring to get in. Is the deadness of many churches and individuals due to the fact that he has been edged out? In Revelation 4:5 the brightly blazing lamps are set before the throne of God. The golden lamp-stand in the Tabernacle leads our thoughts right to Jesus.

GOD'S TENT

Imagine the main screened courtyard, measuring about 150 feet long by 75 feet broad with the screen seven and a half feet high. At the western end is set the Tabernacle itself, measuring roughly 45 feet long, 15 feet wide and 15 feet high. When the tribes of Israel were encamped in their allotted places around the whole structure they would be able to see the actual Tabernacle well above the height of the surrounding wall or screen. Try to think of a surrounding wall within which stands a large marquee. The length of the curtains indicates that they not only covered the sides but that they met over the top. Entering the 'tent', the first section is about 30 feet long and the second about 15 feet long, separated off by a special curtain. That curtain or veil barred the way into the holiest place of all, the very presence of God. Various commentators see in the colours symbols of Christ's divinity, humanity, and royalty, with the scarlet speaking of his sacrifice. The curtains and coverings are described from the inside outwards, perhaps indicating that the whole plan of salvation begins in the secret heart of God and works outward to sinners. The beautiful inner curtain was spread right over the flat roof of the Sanctuary (vv.1-6) and was covered with rougher protective material (vv.7-13). From the outside this symbol of worship and salvation must have seemed unattractive but from inside the true glory would be seen. It is the same with stained glass windows in a church. You cannot see the beauty unless you go inside. It is when Christ brings us 'inside' that we begin to see and enjoy the varied beauties of his salvation and life.

GOD'S PLAN

Before deciding that these detailed passages are dull and of no use to us, note in verse 30 that all had to be according to God's revealed plan. Remember also what all this must have meant to the Israelites for whom symbolism was something very real. When the Tabernacle was erected in the wilderness the supports were not simply sunk into the desert sand but were set into sockets of silver. Some suggest we should see here a symbol of humanity (wood) resting on redemption (silver). When Peter wrote about not being redeemed by silver and gold but by the sacrificial death of Christ (1 Pet. 1:18-19) he may well have been thinking of the details of the Tabernacle. The precise measurements and the instructions about clasps, frames and rings (vv.1-14) may have something to do with the speed and efficiency with which the whole structure could be erected and taken down in the course of Israel's journeys. The details also point forward to what the New Testament teaches about the 'body', the 'building', the 'dwelling-place' for God, where God meets with his people. In Exodus 26:6, 11 we were told of the essential unity of all the different parts. The many parts were to be perfectly measured and fitted into one another to make a unified and stable structure. Read Ephesians 2:18-22; 4:11-16; 1 Corinthians 12:12-25. The picture is that of many made one, fitted together, each contributing to the other and dependent on each other, making an ordered whole which is for the service and glory of another. How much the Israelites knew of the details we cannot say, nor can we say how much they saw during the actual erection of the structure, but the finished Tabernacle must have impressed them with a sense of awe and even mystery. They would be aware of God's presence among them and of how much there was to discover and learn about his plan of salvation. We must never think we know it all.

THE HOLIEST PLACE

e are told here of the inner veil that screened off the 'Most Holy Place' (vv.31-34) and of the screen or curtain that served as the 'outside door' of the

Tabernacle, the holy place (v.36). Keep in mind that the priests entered into the first 'compartment' of the Tabernacle regularly to carry out their religious duties but only the High Priest, and only once a year on the Day of Atonement, would enter the holiest place of all. In Hebrews 9:1-14 we see how wonderfully the pattern of the Tabernacle foreshadowed the atoning death of Jesus, our great High Priest. The inner veil was a veil of exclusion, making it perfectly clear that sinful man had no right of entrance into the holy presence of God. The ritual sacrifices which had to be observed frequently, and the Day of Atonement sacrifice which happened once every year, all signified that sin had not yet been dealt with finally. But they pointed forward to the day when the true Passover Lamb would come and would die to make full and perfect atonement for sin once for all (Heb. 9:23-26). When Jesus died this veil in the Temple in Jerusalem was torn open from the *top* to the bottom (Matt. 27:45-51). It was God's doing not man's, and it signified not just that the price of sin was paid and that atonement had been made, but that forgiven sinners could now come to God and enjoy fellowship and life with him. Note that the sockets for the pillars at the entrance were set in bases of bronze (brass), the same material as the altar for burnt offerings and the laver. The bronze or brass speaks of judgement, and God's judgement on sin is seen in the Cross (Num. 21:4-9; John 3:14-15).

THE PRICE OF SIN

T he bronze altar for sacrifice would be the first thing an Israelite would see as he entered the courtyard of the Tabernacle. This was a reminder that approach to God was possible only on the basis of effective and appointed sacrifice. The sinner approaching to worship had to bring an animal for sacrifice, a substitute for himself. The 'innocent' animal would be tied to the horns at the corners of the altar, and would die for the guilty one. The animal was slain by the priest because the sacrifice was not something the sinner could do for himself. It had to be done by God's appointed man. We are not given these details here but in Leviticus 1:3-4 we are told that the worshipper would lay his hand on the animal, identifying himself with the sacrifice, thus signifying the transfer of his sin to the sacrifice. This altar points us to Jesus, the willing victim who paid the price of sin. But in his sacrifice for sin our Lord Jesus Christ was not dragged like a frightened animal to be bound to the altar. He laid down his life of his own free will (John 10:17-18) and it was his redeeming love and not the nails that bound him to the Cross. Read the wonderful verses in Isaiah 53:4-7, 10-12. Think of the words of the hymn 'Man of Sorrows!':

In my place condemned He stood,
Sealed my pardon with His blood.[25]

Think of the story in Genesis 22:7-8, which tells how Abraham was prepared to sacrifice his son Isaac, and how he made the glorious affirmation that God would provide the lamb for sacrifice. God spared not even his own Son but gave him up for us all (Rom. 8:32).

27:9-21

APPROACH TO GOD

As they approached the courtyard in which the actual Tabernacle was set the people would see the courtyard curtains made of plain fine linen and then, at the entrance, the royal colours of blue, purple and scarlet. They would have been able to look through the opening, which was 30 feet wide, and catch a glimpse of the brilliance of bronze, silver and gold. At the same time they would be very aware of the barrier of the altar of sacrifice. There was only one way into God's presence.

The outer 'wall' of the Tabernacle was made of white linen hangings supported on sixty pillars. These indicated the holiness of Him who dwelt within, in marked contrast to the unholiness of the people who 'tented' or 'tabernacled' all around Him. A holy God in the midst of an unholy people! The 'walls' spoke too of the principle of inclusion and exclusion; within was the sacred space where all that pertained to God was executed, while outside all that was secular was carried out. The sinners outside were separated from the Throne of the Lord – the Throne of Mercy and Grace – by three 'gates'. First, the door to the outer court illustrated the great distance between the sinner and God, but this was shortened by the sacrifices on the bronze altar. Once sprinkled with the blood of the victim, the priest-sinner could then go through the second 'gate' into the Holy Place, but even he was permanently separated from entering the Holy of Holies by the third 'gate' – the veil.[26]

In some ways the message of the Tabernacle was very solemn and yet it spoke of the God who was there, who dwelt with his people, and who had made provision for them to come near to him and to dwell with him. In verses 20-21 we are told of the light that was to burn continually just in front of the veil: a reminder that there was a way to God which was not yet open. In due time the light of the glory of God would shine in the face of Jesus (2 Cor. 4:6; John 8:12).

GOD'S PRIESTS

In the whole pattern of worship priests were needed and these were appointed by God. They did not take it upon themselves to be the representatives of the people in relation to God (Heb. 5:1-4). Aaron and his sons, not Moses, were called to this task. The Israelites would recognise Aaron as one of themselves, sharing their common life and having an understanding of their needs, hopes, fears and failures. In the fullness of time there came our great High Priest, Jesus himself, and he too was 'one of us' in the fullest possible sense (Heb. 2:14-18; 4:14-16). The priests were to act as representatives of the people and as mediators to stand between the people and a holy God. In the gospel era we do not need a system of priests, for there is one Mediator, whose name is Jesus (1 Tim. 2:5), and he is totally and eternally competent. The priests serving in the Tabernacle were to wear garments of glory and beauty to express the high dignity of their office, *not* to signify their personal importance, for they were sinners like the rest of the people. When we reach chapter 32 we will read of how Aaron was involved in the incident of the Golden Calf.

The priests were sinner priests, chosen by sovereign grace to represent their sinner nation before God. It was God's choice which raised them very high both in the sight of God and of the people.... The Aaronic priesthood ended during the Passion of Jesus when the high priest rent his garments – an action expressly forbidden by the Law (Matt. 26:65; Lev. 21:10). This, coupled with the rending of the veil in the Temple, signalled the ending of the Sinaitic Covenant, its priesthood and its sacrificial system.[27]

It is thrilling to see in verse 3 that, in this very important spiritual institution, ordinary people with skill in using needle and thread had a vital part to play. They had a task that God had fitted them for. Read 1 Corinthians 12:12-27, especially verse 22.

28:6-14

AARON'S MINISTRY

The different items of the 'uniform' were listed in verse 4 and now details are given. Pictures or illustrations of the High Priest dressed for duty can be found in some Bible Dictionaries. The materials and colours mentioned are similar to those in the Tabernacle and again may symbolise the divinity, royalty, humanity and purity of our great High Priest the Lord Jesus Christ. The ephod, an outer garment, seems to have been a tunic or apron of two pieces joined at the shoulders and bound round the waist with a band which was woven into the garment and not a separate belt. This girdle round the waist speaks of readiness for service. Think of Jesus when he girded himself with the towel to wash the disciples' feet (John 13:1-5). He came to serve, not to be served (Luke 12:37; 22:24-27; Mark 10:42-45) and we are called to follow his example. The gold chains and filigree settings were for the two precious stones on which were engraved the names of the twelve tribes of Israel. When the High Priest entered the presence of God he carried on his shoulders the people he represented. This is what our Saviour does for us. On the mighty shoulders of his eternal strength, strength that never wearies, he bears our names before the Father. 'He pleads our cause at God's right hand, omnipotent to save.'[28] Read passages such as Romans 8:31-34 and Isaiah 9:6-7; Luke 15:1-7. The ephod seems to emphasise the strength of the High Priest and it speaks of the power of Christ to uphold and to carry his people. What a comfort and encouragement this is when the road ahead seems rough, steep and demanding. The Scottish Paraphrase of Isaiah 40:27-31 speaks wonderfully to the heart:

> Art thou afraid his power shall fail
> when comes thy evil day?
> And can an all-creating arm
> grow weary or decay?[29]

Think often of the One who carries you and who keeps your going out and coming in (Ps. 121:8).

THE SYMPATHISING JESUS

The breastpiece, of similar materials to the ephod, was folded double to make a pouch and it was slung from the shoulders of the ephod. It was a perfect square (vv.15-16), signifying perfection of arrangement and equality. Set in it were twelve separate and distinct precious stones, with different glowing colours, each with the name of one of the tribes of Israel. God's people are all different but are all equally precious, important and entrusted with a specified place in God's plan and service. In verse 28 we see that there was no risk of the breastpiece coming loose. Everything to do with salvation is sure and secure. Picture the High Priest entering God's presence. He carried the people on his shoulders and also on his heart. Strength alone can be a somewhat cold and comfortless thing even though it gives enabling. But strength that has a heart of tender compassion and care is a mighty shelter indeed. Remember that God has called us by name (Isa. 43:1-4a); that our names are graven on the palms of his hands (Isa. 49:14-16); and that we are loved with an everlasting love (Jer. 31:3) by the God who, in spite of all our folly, sin and backsliding, simply refuses to let us go (Hos. 11:1-4, 7-9). Think of Jesus in the wonderful statement in John 13:1 (AV and NIV footnote). Think of Jesus who ever lives to make intercession for us (Heb. 7:25) and who, when we sin, acts as our advocate with the Father (1 John 2:1). When we think of the glories of our great High Priest and the effectiveness of his ministry on our behalf, we must not forget his true and full humanity. He is one who is in fact and experience touched with the feeling of our infirmities (Heb. 4:15 AV). In modern translations that verse says that he sympathises 'with our weaknesses' because he knows what it is to be tempted 'in every way' (in all points). He feels for us and with us. It should be easy to tell him how things really are with us. If we do, he tells the Father.

28:15-30

GUIDANCE

The words 'the means of making decisions' ('for judgment' AV and RSV) in relation to the breastpiece (vv.15, 29) refer to God's guidance to the people when issues had to be settled and decisions made. The two rather mysterious objects called Urim and Thummim were to be carried in the fold of the breastpiece, over Aaron's heart, as were the jewels symbolising the tribes of Israel. Commentators say the names, which are plural, mean 'lights' and 'perfections' and some suggest there may be reference to God's light and truth which, in the metrical version of Psalm 43, speak of guidance: 'O send thy light forth and thy truth; let them be guides to me.'[30] We can only speculate (and that is not very profitable) as to whether one object was white and the other black and whether the answer to the query for guidance was yes or no depending on which stone was drawn from the breastpiece. We must not think in terms of drawing lots, or luck, or chance. We are in the realm of God guiding his people in matters of importance, and there is nothing fickle about God. An example of consulting Urim and Thummim is found in 1 Samuel 14:41 (RSV and NIV footnote), while a warning against consulting 'spirits' or 'mediums' is found in Deuteronomy 18:9-14. Keep in mind that the function of the Priest was also to teach the people (Deut. 33:8-10) and it is as we learn what God is like, and as we come to know God, that guidance becomes a natural part of our lives and not an agonising crisis measure. These verses in Exodus remind us of God's desire to guide us in the right paths. Read Isaiah 30:18-21. If we need guidance and if we *want* guidance we should ask God in the name of the One who carries us in his heart. It can also help to ask some trusted and older believer whose experience as well as knowledge can give wisdom. The real difficulty in guidance lies in our preconceived ideas and the tendency to commit ourselves to a course of action before we seek the mind and will of God. God is not the author of confusion or uncertainty. We need to learn to wait on him, and for him.

28:31-35

SIGHTS AND SOUNDS

The long flowing robe of the High Priest seems to have been woven without seam and put on by slipping it over the head. There may be significance in the robe being seamless, pointing either to the perfect and flawless life of our Lord Jesus or to the endless, continuing ministry he exercises on our behalf. The emphasis on the seamless robe in John 19:23-24 is a clear indication that Jesus was indeed God's true High Priest. The upper part of the robe was to be covered by the ephod but the lower part, which probably reached to the ankles, would by its bright blue colour and its specific ornamentation be a focus of interest to the people. The bottom fringe of the garment was adorned with pomegranates made of soft material alternating with small bells of gold. The pomegranates were symbols of fruitfulness but were also practical in allowing the bells to ring with a clear tone by preventing them from clashing together. The bells too had a practical function. When the High Priest entered the presence of God with the blood of the sacrifice on the Day of Atonement, how were the people to know that all was well? How were they to know that the ritual was being carried out and that their representative had not been struck dead by being in the presence of the awesome holiness of God? As he moved about, the tinkling of the bells would bear testimony that the work was being done. The people could not see into the holy shrine but the sound of the bells would enable them to focus on and identify with what was being done on their behalf and they would worship and be glad. Think how the bread and wine in a Communion Service help us to focus our thoughts and hearts specifically on the death of the Saviour and our acceptance in him. There may be a hint about the bells when we sing the metrical version of Psalm 89:15-18: 'O greatly blessed the people are, the joyful sound that know.'[31]

28:36-39

'HOLY TO THE LORD'

The mitre, turban, or head-dress was made of white linen and seems to have been different from all other head-wear. Its most significant part was the plate of pure gold fastened to it with the inscription, 'HOLY TO THE LORD'. The priest had to be holy: set apart for God, and holy in life. The people had to be holy, because God is holy. All the service and worship of the Tabernacle had to be holy, worthy of the great name of God. Worship and ceremony, however meticulously ordered, even in accordance with Scripture, are neither worthy nor acceptable unless accompanied by true holiness of life. This theme is taken up in 1 Peter 1:13-16. In all the preaching of the gospel there must be this call to holiness of life: a life that is worthy (Eph. 4:1); a light that shines (Phil. 2:14-15); a life that glorifies God (Rom.15:6; 1 Cor. 6:18-20). The Psalmist tells us that offering praise glorifies God (Ps. 50:23 AV) and that God inhabits, and is enthroned upon, the praise of his people (Ps. 22:3, AV and RSV). We must not dare to provide such a throne made of cheap, careless and unworthy materials. The worship of God calls for and deserves the best of all our capacities and gifts. Note in the passage how clearly it is stated that the God-appointed High Priest takes upon himself the guilt attaching to any defects in the offerings of the people. All that we say, and do and give is acceptable to God only in the name and by the merit of the great High Priest who died for us. Whether dedicating our offerings or presenting our prayers, we ask always to be accepted 'for Jesus' sake'. However difficult this chapter has been to study in its mass of detail, there has been one clear result. It has pointed us to the all-sufficient Jesus.

DRESSED FOR CHURCH

aron's sons who were to serve in the priesthood were to be clothed in garments of plain white linen, and yet these clothes were for dignity and honour. It is clear from the description that the clothes were basically practical and, although tunics, sashes and headbands are mentioned, more details are given of the undergarments. This emphasises the need for seemliness in everything to do with the worship and service of God's House. These details are not surprising when you think of the nakedness, indecency and sensuality of much of the pagan worship that surrounded the Israelites and dominated the culture and life of many nations. Nowadays people tend to say that clothes do not matter and that how you dress for church is not important. But clothes can be an indication of a person's attitude, and what may be acceptable and appropriate or fashionable in the life of society is not necessarily right for the House of God. We must be careful in dress and in behaviour not to stir feelings in others that might lead them into temptation. If we look back to the prohibition in Exodus 20:26 we see a clear indication of the nature of what is being emphasised in today's verses. Teaching on the matter of dress has led some to such an extreme of trying not to seem 'worldly' that they have become oddities. This has the result of simply drawing attention to themselves. It certainly does not point to Jesus, nor does it commend him. But there needs to be seemliness. Dress and behaviour must be appropriate for the occasion. Yes, we stand in the liberty of Christ and the gospel (Gal. 5:1). Yes, God looks on the heart not the outward appearance (1 Sam. 16:7). Yes, we must guard against the hypocrisy of the Pharisees whose religion was all outward, and conditioned by what people would think (Matt. 6:1-5, 16-18). But worthiness and respect for holy things are important.

29:1-9

SET APART FOR GOD

If we tend to grow weary of these chapters in Exodus we should remember two things. All Scripture is given by inspiration of God. It is God-breathed and it is profitable for our training for service (2 Tim. 3:16-17). We would not have these chapters if they were not necessary. Perhaps we, like the Israelites, have much to learn about the spirit in which we approach God. We are told in Luke 24:25-27 that Jesus rebuked the disciples after his resurrection because they had failed to see the truth about his Person and work in the books of Moses. Of course the truths of salvation are given here in shadowy form: hints, indications and symbolic presentations, because that was all the people were able to receive at that stage of their spiritual experience and education. As they were able, they had to learn about God, his holiness, his laws and demands, his attitude to and his way of dealing with sin. They had to learn how to be God's redeemed people and what God required of his people in terms of life, worship, service and witness. In teaching children we use verbal instruction and visual aids. That is exactly what God was doing for his people in the details of the Tabernacle, its worship and its sacrifices. Here the lesson being learned is that God chooses and sets apart some for particular spiritual service. God chose Aaron and his sons. God ordained the nature of their religious garments. Now God commanded the pattern of their public consecration to service, which had to be carried out by Moses. God's act and man's act are seen together. A similar scene is recorded in Acts 13:1-4, where the work of the Holy Spirit and the work of the leaders of the church are seen to be in total harmony. The priests were brought to the door of the Tabernacle and ceremonially washed. Those who do God's work must be clean (Isa. 52:11).

HOLY SERVICE

The various sacrifices in the Old Testament all point in some way to different aspects of the sacrifice of Christ and if we take time to ponder these passages we shall see different facets of the gospel and of the life of the Christian believer. In verses 1-3 we are told of the sacrifice by which the priests were consecrated. Then there is the washing clean (v.4), followed by the anointing with oil (v.7). If we are to serve God, we must first be right with God ourselves. This means we must be in right relationship with Jesus Christ and him crucified, not just in terms of the forgiveness of sins and justification, but in terms of taking up the Cross, denying self, and following him. Jesus spoke of this way of life and so did Paul (Matt. 16:24-26; Phil. 3:7-1l). When we come to Christ we are washed clean from our sins (cf. Isa. 1:18). But as well as that once-for-all cleansing there is the ongoing cleansing spoken of in 1 John 1:5-10. It is in this way that we maintain our walk with God, and if this is neglected because of sin unconfessed and unforgiven, then our service is in danger. Even if sin does not close our lips our words will not ring true. Think of David's heart cry in Psalm 51:4-15. It was his service, not his salvation, that was in danger. It is the clean servant who is able to tell others. For all service there is need for the anointing of the Holy Spirit, typified here in the reference to the oil in verse 7. To preach and teach without the life-giving unction of the Holy Spirit is vain indeed. We cannot *be* Christians without having the Holy Spirit dwelling in us (Rom. 8:9-11). But the Spirit can be grieved and quenched in terms of service (Eph. 4:29-32; 1 Thess. 5:19). The activity of the Spirit is linked by Paul to the prayers of the people (Phil. 1:19). Serving God in the gospel is a serious business.

29:10-21

COSTLY FORGIVENESS

Do not be distracted by the rather grim details of the sacrifices but keep in mind that they demonstrate that forgiveness of sin does not come easily. The bull was the sin offering and the hands laid on it typify the passing of guilt from the person to the offering. The sin-offering dies (v.11) and the sinner is pardoned and reconciled. Think of Paul's startling words in 2 Corinthians 5:21 speaking of how Jesus was made sin for us, identified with the evil thing in all its offence to God, in order that we might be made righteous. These grim sacrifices described here should help us to grasp something of the terribleness of the price of sin. Perhaps we should ask ourselves if we find the details of sacrifice more distasteful than the thought of sin. Some of the blood was put on the horns of the altar, perhaps in relation to those who would in desperation run and cling to the horns of the altar for mercy (Exod. 21:12-14; cf. 1 Kgs 2:28). The bulk of the carcass was burned outside the camp of Israel, perhaps signifying that sin was like a leprosy and had no place in the life of God's people. Even the reference to 'outside the camp' points to Jesus who suffered outside the city (Heb. 13:11-12). The sacrifice of the bull is spoken of in Leviticus 8:14-15 in terms of atonement for sin. The first ram is a burnt offering (Lev. 8:18), an offering by fire to the Lord, in relation to the injury done to him by human sin, an aspect of sin we tend to forget. The second ram is described in verse 22 and again in Leviticus 8:22 in terms of ordination. It is a token of the offering of lives to God for service. The touching of ears, hands and toes speaks of all the faculties and capacities being dedicated to God: the ear for the hearing and receiving of God's Word; the hand as the instrument of service; and the foot representing the holy walk of obedience.

THE WAVE OFFERING

Following the solemn consecration of the priests the ritual of ordination continued with the wave offering. The meat and bread being offered were placed in the hands of Aaron and his sons. This may signify that the priests in their service would be provided for by the sanctuary (cf. 1 Cor. 9:3-14). Note how in verses 27-28 the offering of the people for the support of the priests is spoken of as being offered to the Lord. There has been great emphasis on the sacrificial nature of the total commitment of the priests to their God-given task, but now the emphasis is on the generous and continuing provision God makes for his servants. Remember Jesus' answer to Peter when he impetuously spoke of how much he had given up (Matt. 19:27-30). God is no man's debtor. But then, in the wave offering, the priests declared that all that was given them by God was given back to God. It is good to remember that all we have that is worth giving, we have in fact received from God. There is no room for pride, and certainly no room for comparing ourselves favourably with others (1 Cor. 4:7). The hereditary succession of Aaron's sons to the priesthood is emphasised in verses 29-30. The rest of the passage speaks of a holy meal at which the priests eat of the very things by which atonement was made (v.33).

This must surely speak of the believer's participation in Christ's death and resurrection and we can think of it in terms of the Communion Service: 'Take, eat, this is my body which was broken for you.' The New Testament speaks of partaking of the divine nature so that Christ's life becomes our life (2 Pet. 1:3-4). But this is reserved for God's own people. It is made very plain that an outsider shall not eat at this feast. The blessings of the gospel can never be enjoyed by those who choose to stay outside in unbelief. Nor can the blessings of the gospel be truly enjoyed by those who, although they are part of the church, choose to stay aloof, on the edge of both the fellowship and the service of the congregation. It is only in the fellowship of believers that we begin to understand and enjoy the love of Christ that is beyond measurement (Eph. 3:14-19).

29:35-46

GOD WITH US

The service of consecration dealt not only with the priests but also with the altar. The meaning of the last phrase of verse 37 is vague. It cannot mean that mere touching of the altar would make someone or something holy. Ellicott suggests it has the meaning of 'must be holy'.[32] That seems to fit in with the general emphasis of sanctification in relation to God's service. The daily sacrifices seem to have been in connection with the daily sins of the nation and a reminder of the need for renewed, daily self-dedication. We could link this with Romans 12:1-2 in terms of an ongoing presenting of our bodies as a living sacrifice, which is our reasonable and spiritual worship. In verse 40 the reference to the elements of an ordinary meal suggests that all we mean by 'ordinary' daily life is part of our offering to God. Now consider what has been the great objective in the mind and heart of God in and through all this elaborate sacrificial ritual. Sin was to be dealt with so that God the Lord could dwell in happy harmony with his people, so that he and they could both enjoy the experience. Holy communion is a wonderful phrase. It speaks of happy harmony in which no shadows of any kind fall. Note how clear God is about it all. He will dwell with his people. He will meet with them and speak with them, and, as a true Father, he will want to hear his children's voices. He is not ashamed to be called their God (Heb. 11:16). The very building of the Tabernacle will be sanctified by God's glory. God cannot be in his house without his glory being there. If God was pleased to give us eyes to see, then we would see as Isaiah did, and would no doubt react in the same staggering way as he did (Isa. 6:1-8). What a thrill, blessing and inspiration it is to become aware that we are in fact God's people, and that we are so because he has chosen and redeemed us

(Eph. 1:3-8). How we need to remember that we are a people redeemed and saved out of a life of bondage. Our gratitude should remove all reluctance in terms of service (1 Pet. 2:9-10; Col. 1:9-14).

PRAYER

The altar spoken of in the previous chapter was the one that stood at the entrance to the courtyard. Now we are dealing with a different one, the altar of incense which stood in the holy place just in front of the veil that screened off the inner shrine, the Holy of Holies, the symbol of God's presence. In Hebrews 9:3-4 the incense altar is spoken of as being set in the most holy place and there is no explanation of this seeming contradiction, except that the smoke of the incense, which so often in Scripture is a symbol of prayer (Rev. 8:3-4, Luke 1:8-10), would have penetrated into the most holy place through the curtain or veil. It is not difficult, indeed it is easy, to think in terms of the High Priestly ministry of our Lord Jesus Christ. He prays endlessly for us. We sing the Scottish Paraphrase of Hebrews 4:14ff.:

He who for men their surety stood,
And poured on earth His precious blood,

Pursues in heaven His mighty plan,
The Saviour and the friend of man.[33]

We must hold together the objective fact of the
Saviour's atoning death, the death he died once-for-all,
never to be repeated, and his ongoing work in Heaven as
Intercessor and Advocate. The reference in verse 10
about making atonement for the actual altar certainly
seems to suggest that all we mean by the heavenly
intercession of Christ is based on his work of atonement.
Of course, the priest in Israel offered prayer on behalf of
the people and we may see in the incense the rising up of
our prayers, which prayers are presented at the throne of
God in the name of and by the merit of the Jesus who
died for us. The verses from Revelation, quoted earlier
in this note, speak of the prayers of the saints mingling
with the incense. The incense of the prayers of Jesus our
High Priest and our poor stumbling prayers mingle
together until it is not possible to distinguish the two.
What an encouragement to pray! We are told that the
Holy Spirit helps and enables us in our praying (Rom.
8:26) so that our limited words, our heartaches and
longings are interpreted and presented in perfect form
to God. Let your heart thrill to Hebrews 7:25.

MONEY

The atonement money is the same as the tribute money collected by the officials of the Temple in Jesus' day (Matt. 17:24-27), and does not refer to the offerings of the Lord's people Sunday by Sunday. In the people's offerings each must give as the Lord has prospered, and do it with a glad heart (1 Cor. 16:1-2; 2 Cor. 9:7). The value of the gift is measured on God's scale, not man's (Mark 12:41-44). In today's passage each person brought the same half-shekel. It was a practice that put all on the same level before God as to the value of their soul, and reminded each person that the same price was paid for their redemption. The offering did not 'pay' the ransom, but reminded all that they were a people ransomed by God. This is something we in the church need to remember. It is God's church, redeemed by blood that was his own (Acts 20:28). The ransom offering was small and within the capacity of all. If the poor refused to give, it would be a token of their pride and refusal to yield to God. If the rich sought to give more, it would be a token of their pride and self-sufficiency. It seems in verses 11-12 that God ordered the taking of a census to give each person the opportunity to acknowledge his redemption by God. Later experience was to show Israel the danger of seeking to number the people (1Chr. 21:1-8ff.). Once we move into the realm of statistics it is all too easy to focus attention on who we are, what we are, how strong and successful we are. But when that happens we have forgotten this basic principle of today's passage: each person should remind himself or herself that all we have and are able to do is from the grace and mercy of the God who gave his Son to ransom us by his death.

30:17-21

WASHED CLEAN

The last piece of furniture or equipment for the Tabernacle is the bronze basin for ceremonial washing. It stood in the great courtyard and as the priests entered for their various services they came first to the altar of sacrifice and then to the place of washing. Only after being 'cleansed' could they go forward to enter the actual tent to perform their duties. The message of the basin is one of washing clean. The atoning blood of Jesus Christ, God's Lamb, has secured for us eternal redemption (Heb. 9:11-12; John 1:29, 35). All through Scripture, and all through life, we are called to behold the Lamb of God who takes away the sin of the world. But in the course of life and service it is a fact that we sin again and again, and if we seek to deny this then we are foolish liars. But if we confess our sins, we are not just reassured of forgiveness but are told that the blood of Jesus Christ, God's Son, *keeps on* cleansing us from all sin. Read and thrill to 1 John 1:5-10. Read also David's plea to God to be washed through and through so that he would be clean (Ps. 51:2, 7, 10). There is also reference to the washing of water by the Word (Eph. 5:25-27), and Jesus spoke of his disciples being made clean through his Word (John 15:3; 17:17). There are wise words about keeping our lives clean in Psalm 119:9-11. How important it is to keep our lives clean so that we will always be ready to serve the Lord. Clean hands and pure hearts are needed (Ps. 24:3, 4), and in the business of contending for the faith and of witnessing to others, of being a blessing and a help to others in the things of God, we need to keep ourselves unspotted from the worldly world (Jude 20-23). Today's verses make plain that in the service of God we either keep clean or we die out. How rightly the hymn 'Rock of Ages' makes us pray, 'Wash me, Saviour, or I die.'[34]

ANOINTING OIL

The recipe for making the anointing oil is given in great detail and it would be followed meticulously. It was to be in every sense a unique oil, to be used only for its holy purpose, and not secularised in any way (vv.31-33). Anyone who tried to pass off a substitute as the 'real thing' would be cut off from God's people because they would be manifesting a false 'spirit'. In Scripture oil is often a symbol of the Holy Spirit and there are warnings right through the Bible about false spirits and false Christs. All that claims to be spiritual has to be put to the test and not accepted at face value (1 John 4:1; 2 Cor.11:13-15). If the spirit is 'real' then it will point unerringly to Christ, who is supreme, just as all the various pieces of furniture in the Tabernacle point away from themselves to Christ in his Person and perfect work of atonement. The Holy Spirit does not draw attention to himself. He testifies to Christ (John 15:26). Note further how the unique oil was to be applied to every article of furniture and also to Aaron and his sons. This was to consecrate all to the service of God. The lesson seems obvious. All service, however much it is conformed to God's Word, is lifeless apart from the life-giving unction of the Holy Spirit. It is the Spirit who gives life (John 6:63). But it is not simply the power of the Holy Spirit that is symbolised here. Think of the myrrh, cinnamon, aromatic cane and cassia (vv.23-25), and consider the fragrance that must have resulted from the anointing with this oil. There would be a 'sweet smelling savour' (2 Cor. 2:14-16, AV) in the Tabernacle: the fragrance of the presence of the Saviour God.

30:34-38

WITNESS

The theme of fragrance is continued in these specific instructions about the incense. The fragrance of the anointing oil, together with that of the incense, rises up to God as a pleasing scent or remembrance of Christ. We have already considered the incense in relation to prayer, and now prayer is spoken of in terms of sweetness. There is an emphasis on the sweetness of worship offered to God for his pleasure. He sees his children 'in Christ' and thus sees of the travail of his soul and is satisfied. Think of God the Father looking at the Cross of his Son and then looking at the company of ransomed 'children' gathered in his presence for worship, because they have responded to redeeming love. The Father would say, 'It was worth the cost.' Christ is spoken of as the Rose of Sharon (Song 2:1) and it is true that as we company with him his fragrance 'attaches' to us so that wherever we go we carry with us, unconsciously, the fragrance of Christ. Think how smoke in public places can stick to our clothes in an objectionable way for a long time, even after we have stopped noticing it. The touch of Christ, by the Holy Spirit, 'attaches' to us and makes us witnesses to him. But, to use other metaphors, we must not let the light be shadowed (Matt. 5:14-16), nor allow the salt to lose its tang (Matt. 5:13). There is a solemn as well as an encouraging aspect to carrying the sweet fragrance of Christ in the world. In 2 Corinthians 2:14-16 we are told that at one and the same time we are an 'aroma' of Christ to those being saved and to those being lost. The reaction can be so very different but our responsibility is to make sure our lives are giving the right message. We must also make sure that our congregational life and worship convey a true sense of the presence, the holiness and the redeeming love of God.

31:1-11

PRACTICAL SERVICE

The detailed plans for the Tabernacle and its fitments have been given, and chosen men have been set apart for specific holy duties in relation to worship. But everything had to be made and put together and that too is holy and spiritual work. To this practical fabric work God called specific people by name, Bezalel (v.2) and Oholiab (v.6), two men about whom nothing much is known apart from their skill as tradesmen. They may not have had good education and university degrees, but they were the people needed for and vital to the holy work of God. They, along with many colleagues, were men of capacity and calibre, true craftsmen able to work with their hands to fulfil detailed plans. We must note particularly that the gifts and capacities of these men are spoken of as being the gifts of the Holy Spirit. They may have had what we would call natural ability, but not all so endowed are ready and willing to do this kind of 'ordinary' manual work which never takes the front of the stage in the life of the Tabernacle or the church. The gifts of the Spirit that are popular today are generally the more demonstrative kind, the seemingly 'spiritual' kind that tend to draw attention to the person. These men spoken of here were, in the very best sense, what would be called 'church workers', and not all who claim to be evangelical and spiritual can claim to be workers. Note too that along with all the precious metal and material work, these men also made the anointing oil and the fragrant incense (v.11). Would there not be a gracious unction upon these men, who may well have regarded themselves as the ordinary ones of the congregation? Far too often in the work of our churches we undervalue and forget those who do the inglorious work behind the scenes. If they are off ill we may be astonished at how much the rest of us have to do. If they are absent, we are aware something is missing.

OBEDIENCE

The closing verse of the passage emphasises that all the detailed Spirit-inspired and Spirit-enabled work had to be carried out according to all that God had commanded. This is a necessary caution, because fallen human nature always tends to demand the kind of liberty that allows it to express itself, however and whenever it chooses. In the same way some who feel themselves particularly inspired by the Holy Spirit tend to assume that they may act without restriction or correction. But the proof that a person truly belongs to God in Jesus Christ and serves God 'in the Spirit' is obedience. Jesus made this perfectly clear when he said, '1f you love me, you will obey what I command' (John 14:15). Of course, even for Christians, obedience does not always come easily. There is a death to die to self-will and self-pleasing that is costly and is an essential element in discipleship (Matt. 16:24-26). But it is in that very 'death' that liberty, direction and fulfilment of personality are found. George Matheson the hymn-writer grasped this clearly when he wrote:

> Make me a captive, Lord.
> And then I shall be free; ...
>
> My heart is weak and poor
> Until it master find;
> It has no spring of action sure–
> It varies with the wind....
>
> My will is not my own
> Till Thou hast made it Thine;
> If it would reach a monarch's throne
> It must its crown resign.[35]

These are truths we need to remember when we resent the limitations of circumstances and feel they are preventing us being what we want to be. There is a freedom in surrender to the will of God. Jesus expressed it simply: 'Not as I will, but as you will' (Matt. 26:36-44).

31:12-18

GOD'S PATTERN FOR LIFE

he theme of glad obedience to the good and perfect will of God is the right introduction to this passage which emphasises the importance of God's Sabbath. It is not clear why the word in verse 13 is plural, unless it refers to the ongoing weekly Sabbath down through the generations. An immense amount of work had to be done in preparing and erecting the Tabernacle and if enthusiasm was kindled it would have been all too easy for the workers simply to go on and on, with the result that even while doing God's work they could have forgotten God. The Sabbath of rest from work was ordained and commanded as a necessary spiritual exercise and blessing so that the people of God would he reminded that they were in fact God's people, and the objects of his particular choice. The Sabbath was to be a sign, a particular and significant sign, that would mark out the people as God's people, doing God's will. The Sabbath was instituted at Creation (Gen. 2:2-3) and has to be seen as an essential part of God's order of things. It is not incidental, and we have the personal example of God himself to follow (v.17). Note that rest and refreshment are of the essence of the Sabbath. It is for our good, physically, emotionally and spiritually, that we are commanded to keep the Sabbath for God and not to allow things to encroach that will cloud our awareness of God and in a subtle, almost unnoticed way, draw us away from God. The solemnity of verse 14 makes plain that God is speaking of those who will make a specific decision not to go his way, and who in doing so refuse to accept the 'sign' that marks them out as being God's redeemed people. What we do with our

Sundays should mark us out as being different from the people of the world, but not in a cold, legalistic condemnatory way.

THE GOLDEN CALF

These verses reveal just how fickle and shallow minds and hearts can be. Even those who claim to be God's redeemed people can quickly and radically turn away from God in the most profane, carnal and blasphemous way. Look back to Exodus 24:7-8, 15-18 and recall the great vow of consecration made by the people, and how they saw the glory of God settled on the mountain. These were times of great spiritual significance for the people in relation to their future life and service in the purposes of God. But for nearly seven weeks the people were not allowed to be 'in on' the private meeting between Moses and God. They had been told to wait upon God, but there was no thrill in that, and even the cloud of God's glory on the mountain had remained so steady that it had lost its attraction and impact. The people grew weary. There was nothing exciting or stimulating about this kind of spiritual life. They craved for something that would excite, thrill and satisfy. It is quite alarming to see that so soon after the personal leadership and spiritual influence of Moses were out of the situation the people moved so far away from God. Had they leaned more on Moses than on God? Had their commitment been formal and superficial rather than true and radical? The contempt for Moses expressed in verse 1 tends to shock us but we must remember what we read earlier of how these people had grumbled against Moses whenever difficulties or dangers threatened their safety or satisfaction (Exod. 15:24; 17:1-3). What we must certainly see here is a deliberate and specific stratagem of the Devil, attacking the work by side-tracking the people of God at a very significant stage in the work. We must never forget the Devil (Eph. 6:10ff.; 1 Pet. 5:8). Watch and pray (Matt. 26:41).

32:1-6

COMPROMISE

Aaron's part in this tragic situation is sad. He had been left in charge of the people in Moses' absence: a privilege and responsibility. He was not a spiritual novice. He had been Moses' spokesman (Exod. 4:10-16) and Moses' fellow intercessor (Exod. 17:8-12). At this very time he was being marked out by God as High Priest for the people (Exod. 28:1-2). It was little wonder that the Devil was after him (cf. Luke 22:31-34). It is clear

Aaron was neither on guard nor prepared for this spiritual crisis. It seems from verse 1 that the people were aware that Aaron was the kind of man who could be pressurised into doing what he might not have wanted to do, and we have here an example of how congregations can blackmail a minister into spiritual compromise. It is easy to criticise Aaron, but spiritual leadership involves being 'out front' and that is a very lonely and vulnerable place humanly speaking. Perhaps Aaron was seeking a solution along the lines of compromise and thought, perhaps, that asking for their gold would make them hesitate. It did not work. The golden calf was made with the gold that should have been reserved for the work of the Tabernacle. There are occasions when *we* give our best time and energy to the world or indeed to the Devil rather than to God! It was the people, not Aaron, who hailed the calf as their god, but it was Aaron who then sought to give the whole thing an aura of spirituality by building an altar and proclaiming a fast. The whole incident is very revealing. The people's lack of faith and shallow spirituality demanded visible signs of God's presence among them. The determination of the congregation to have 'carnal' satisfaction broke the consecration of Aaron (cf. Amos 2:11-12). Faced with intimidation, the interim leader gave way. It is not easy in practice to know when to stand firm and when to give ground, and the only way is to walk closely with God.

GOD WHO SEES

The seriousness of this whole incident is seen in the fact that the story is re-told and commented on in the second giving of the Law in Deuteronomy 9:6-21. We are told here in the plainest of terms that nothing is ever hidden from God (Heb. 4:13). This is wonderful comfort when we are walking with God and we are assured that he knows, understands and feels for us in every joy, sorrow and battle. But when our attitudes and actions are contrary to God it can be a sobering and a saving experience to be reminded that everything, down to the smallest detail, is known to God. Whether we are aware of it or not we live our lives in the presence of God. We are often hesitant to think of God as being angry: angry with his own people and not just angry with the godless and blasphemous heathen. There may be some excuse for the sins of those who live in total darkness and ignorance of God. But for those who have the light of God and who have had the experience of God saving them out of bondage, and blessing them with new life, there is no excuse. We are told here that God was ready to disown his own people. He speaks of them to Moses as *your* people, a people who had been quick to turn aside from their God (cf. Gal. 1:6). God stated that he was ready to give the people what they deserved, and to leave them with the golden idol they had chosen as their god. These people, by their sinful disobedience, had reached the point where they were about to lose their spiritual identity, calling, service and destiny. God was serious. He is not prepared to trifle with the holy things of his purposes of salvation. He will not abandon his plan of salvation, but he was ready to abandon a favoured people and to start all over again. The New Testament comment is in 1 Corinthians 9:24-27 where Paul speaks of being disqualified, or laid aside as of no further use. In 1 Corinthians 10:1-12 we are warned about being over-confident regarding our own spirituality and commitment.

32:11-14

INTERCESSION

We must see very clearly that it was Moses, the man who was despised and rejected, who became the great intercessor on behalf of the people. There is no suggestion that Moses disagreed with God in his evaluation of the people and their inexcusable sin. We must see also the great temptation to personal ambition faced by Moses in God's statement at the end of verse 10. After all, he was a fully human man, just as Jesus was, and for both of them temptation was real

(Luke 4:1-13; Heb. 4:15). The whole story is told in human terms and we must not think of God as tempting Moses to evil, because God does not do that kind of thing (Jas 1:13-15). Nor must we think of God 'changing his mind' in the way we can be prevailed upon to change our minds. Nor should we think of God regretting the stern words he had spoken, and the stern course of action he had intended. 'It means... that [God] now embarked on a different course of action from that already suggested as a possibility, owing to some new factor... mentioned in the context'.[36] The new factor is of course prayer. God's warnings and promises are set in Scripture in the context of man's response and, in the response of intercessory prayer, we see God's purposes working out. It was a wise man who said, 'The prayers of the saints are the decrees of God beginning to work.' Moses' prayer was grounded in a concern for the name of God, his glory and his integrity as the God who had made promises to his people. Moses' prayer was answered. The people down below were not aware that there was someone praying behind the scenes, nor were they aware of how their whole future was undergirded by and dependent on the intercessions of the man they despised. Even while Moses prayed, the disaffected people indulged in revelry they called worship, and in activity that was offensive to God. Moses' prayer was heard and answered, but there were still inescapable consequences.

DAY OF RECKONING

We have seen Moses as a mighty man of prayer, speaking earnestly to God as mediator and intercessor, and his prayer prevailed. We are told of Moses in Numbers 12:3 that he was meek or humble, more than any other man. This makes us think of our Lord Jesus Christ who was meek and lowly in heart (Matt. 11:28-30, AV). But meekness does not imply weakness either in character or spirituality and there is no sentimental softness seen in Moses as he confronted the sinful, rebellious people. Of course he had been enlightened by God as to the situation and therefore he was prepared. He also had in his hand the God-given tables of the Law which carried the authority of God. He was accompanied by Joshua, who was marked out already to be the leader of the people in the future development and advance of God's purposes (Josh. 1:1-5). But Joshua was slow to discern the actual problem. Perhaps he was too innocent and did not think God's favoured and richly blessed people would want to go far wrong. Perhaps he allowed his friendship with and his regard for the people to cloud his spiritual judgement. This is a constant temptation. We can refuse to see people's wrong spirit and actions simply because we like them! Note in verse 18 the reference to the sound of singing. There was hilarity. The people were having fun. They had no awareness of how angry God was with them. In mind, heart and spirit they were no doubt recalling the great times they had had in the enjoyment of worldly Egypt (Num. 11:4-6). When Moses came into the camp he saw at once the focus of the problem: the calf and the dancing. It was worship that was man-inspired, man-made, man-desired, and man-satisfying. It had nothing to do with God or with giving glory to God. It was all man-centred. That was not worship. In our day we must not confuse worship with tradition, nor with any particular order of service or style of music or singing. Archbishop Temple writes:

> Worship is the submission of all our nature to God. It is the quickening of conscience by His holiness; the nourishment of mind with His truth; the purifying of imagination by His beauty; the opening of the heart to His love; the surrender of will to His purpose – and all of this gathered up in adoration, the most selfless emotion of which our nature is capable and therefore the chief remedy for that self-centredness which is our original sin and the source of all actual sin.[37]

NECESSARY JUDGEMENT

The great intercessor, in total harmony with God, was angry, and in symbolic action he threw down the tables of the Law, making clear that the people stood condemned by the broken Law. The later verses of the chapter will indicate that the people were not all impressed or subdued by Moses' action. But there was more to follow. The golden calf was destroyed and the dust of it was scattered. Their sin not only cost *them* their gold; the gold that had been set apart for God had been lost to the work of God. They had stolen from God what was his by right. In the same way the freshness and vitality of our lives can be lost in terms of our service to God by our sinning and backsliding. The people realised that the gold which they had given up so eagerly and without complaint in the interest of their backsliding would never be recovered. In days to come there would be things they would want to give to God and do for God which would be outside their capacity because of what they had done. But the rebuke was not yet complete. The dust of the gold was scattered on the water and the people were made to drink it, as if to remind them that their sin was not something outside or external to their lives and their persons. There may be a suggestion here that certain sexual sins were involved in

the 'dancing rites' of the worship of the golden calf. If
that is so we do well to consider Paul's words in 1
Corinthians 6:12-20 and the serious, practical warning in
James 1:15. Sin is not necessarily finished when the
specific act is over, whatever the act may be. These are
solemn thoughts and lest we be left in despair we need
to remember that it is God who says that sins that are
scarlet can be made white as snow (Isa. 1:18). It is the
God who rebukes and punishes sin who loves his people
in spite of all, refusing to give them up, and promising
to heal their backsliding (Hos. 11:7-9; 14:4, AV).

32: 21 - 29

SIN IS DANGEROUS

Aaron was a man destined by God for
profound spiritual work. But here he is
seen as weak and ineffective when charged
by Moses with having brought great sin
upon the people. Of course Moses knew full well what
the people were like, and he had had problems with
them. Aaron may have felt hard done by that Moses
had left him alone so long with such a difficult
congregation. When faced with the crisis it may have
been that Aaron tried to manoeuvre the people away
from their desires rather than take a stand himself. If
that be so he was doing what Pilate later did at the

arrest of Jesus. It does not work. What Aaron meant by saying, 'Out came this calf' (v.24) is not clear. It had not been a miracle. He had made it (Exod. 32:4). Aaron had blundered, but this great error did not result in his losing his God-given calling. The people had seen him as weak and had taken advantage. When Moses assessed the situation he saw both the nature and the extent of the sin that Aaron's weakness had led to. The people had run wild ('broken loose', AV), and this seems to indicate that in the frantic dancing, so common among idolatrous worshippers at that time and indeed since then, the people had not only cast off restraint but had cast off their clothing. This would not only be to their own shame when they cooled down and came to their senses, it would shame them in the sight of their enemies and cause them to be totally unprepared to face and repel any attack. In every sense sin 'exposes' us to danger and to shame. The picture we have is similar to what is now called a 'rave' and, because the Devil is clever and people are gullible (especially untaught and undisciplined Christians), it is not beyond imagination to consider the possibility of people organising a 'Christian rave'. When religion is mingled with indulgence the mixture is dangerous and can be spiritually lethal.

EVIL DEALT WITH

How many realise that the hymn, 'Who is on the Lord's side?'[38] echoes this story? The people could not say they were ignorant of God's required standards because in Exodus 24:3-4 the people gave assent to the ordinances already promulgated, including the Ten Commandments in 20:1-20. It was therefore to an instructed people who had deliberately flouted God's laws that the challenge was given in verse 26. We must not fail to see that this call to repentance and return was spoken to a people who had transgressed greatly, who had been shown their error, and who had been told of God's anger and rebuke. Moses' own tribe of Levi seems to have responded without hesitation. We cannot tell how many others responded nor can we tell just how many were involved in the original idolatry. That God's judgement was carried out is clear and, although three thousand seems many to us, it may in fact be a comparatively small number out of the many thousands of Israelites. Imagine the awe that must have gripped those who carried out the judgement. Keep in mind that in every movement of spiritual defection there are leaders and there are those who have been beguiled, enticed and drawn in foolishly, because of various involvements and commitments. These are basically different groups and have to be dealt with differently. When God's rebuke is spoken and his discipline exercised, those who are genuine in heart will hurry to God, rebuked and ashamed and no doubt frightened because of what had happened. This they must do in a way that is clear to all, not least to the leader of the work. Those who refuse to stop idolatry and disobedience must be dealt with and rooted out so that they will not continue as a source of spiritual and moral poison within the body of the people and the work. Moses stood in the gate and spoke to all those who had taken themselves outside the camp. The gate was open, but for the impenitent the gate was shut.

32:30-35

THE SINFULNESS OF SIN

o doubt Moses would have been accused of being hard and harsh by some of those who were drawn back by fear, and certainly by the relatives of those who had paid the price of sin in God's judgement. That is always the case when standards are set and discipline is administered, and it is something that all leaders of God's work have to live with. The truth about Moses is seen in that he was prepared to be personally blotted out of God's book of life in order that the people might be spared. He was willing to accept judgement that should have been theirs in order that *they* might be forgiven. Paul expresses the same deep heartache of love in Romans 9:1-5. We cannot but think of Jesus who took our place and died our death so that we might live. When Moses spoke the words of verse 30 we wonder just how many had a true realisation of the enormity of their sin. Perhaps the sinfulness of sin was just beginning to dawn on them. When Moses spoke of his making atonement for their sin had they any idea of what was in his mind and heart? Did they realise that this man who took such a serious view of sin was a man who knew the depth and the cost of true love? Moses, so reviled, despised and rejected, was willing to die for them, and he knew more than any just what atonement cost, because he had been told about it in the revelations of the sacrifices in the Tabernacle worship. Moses' offer, his readiness for self-sacrifice, should make us think deeply of the words in Romans 5:6-11. Moses, who was so stern when he faced sin and rebellion against God was full of tender, agonising love in the presence of God as he pleaded for his people, who were God's people. There was no suggestion of resignation. He was still their shepherd, leader and teacher.

LOST OPPORTUNITY

We must not try to set up a contradiction between what seems to be answered prayer in verse 14 and the agony of intercession in today's passage. The two emphases belong together. Jesus knew quite clearly what he had come into the world to do and how it was to be done (Matt. 16:21-23; John 12:27) even though he prayed with agony in Gethsemane. God's answer to Moses made clear that there was a distinction between forgiveness of sins and facing and living with the consequences of sin. The plan and purpose of God had not been cancelled out. God reserves to himself the right to deal with sin and with sinners, because he alone knows all the facts, the motives and the intentions. God recognises that some have been more sinned against than sinning, and we need to recall Jesus' words about those who cause one of his young disciples to stumble and to fall into error (Luke 17:1-2). Moses was told to go back to the people and to lead them on into the future, just as previous instructions had stipulated. God promised tokens of his presence to go before them. There may be a suggestion that an angel was to be a substitute for God's personal presence, but we must not push that thought too far. What we must see clearly is that that whole generation would yet live with the consequences of their sin. The fulfilment in service that could have been theirs in the land of promise would never come to them. There would be the 40 years of wandering and the refusal by God to allow them to enter the land (Deut. 1:32-36). Far from this being unreasonable and a contradiction of forgiveness, it was in fact necessary. Their idolatry of heart and their unbelief had shown they were incapable of coping with the challenge, the demand and the discipline of conquering the land and displacing the enemies of God. They would have been confounded by their enemies. In a sense God was sparing them. His judgements were mixed with mercy. As they grew older they must often have thought of what might have been, but for their shameful sinning.

_33:1-6_

BREACH OF FELLOWSHIP

Although they had sinned grievously the people were not cast off by God nor had they forfeited their identity and service as the chosen people of God. The faithful promises of God were still valid for them and in their future work God said he would fight for them, vindicate them and drive out their enemies. The possibilities were still there. The destiny and blessing of a land flowing with milk and honey were still held out to them. But they had forfeited one very precious thing. They would not know or be aware of the gracious presence of their God with them and among them. There was to be a change of experience. Sin has consequences and even though the sorrow of the people was indicated by their putting away their ornaments (vv.4, 6) there was to be a narrowing and limiting of fellowship. It could not be otherwise because the heart of their God was grieved because of their sinning. They were deprived of this sweetness of companionship and so was God. In our self-centredness we forget that God has feelings. He can be grieved and disappointed (Isa. 1:2-3; Mic. 6:3-4). But we must see clearly in these verses that it was in order to spare the people that God held himself back from coming amongst them. There was a real limit to what God could give of himself because they would not be able to cope. Think of how earnestly and sometimes emotionally people cry to God to come in reviving power in his church. But who is ready to stand in such a day (Mal. 3:1-3)? The same principle of God's restraint is expressed in Jesus' words in John 16:12. We may have to stay in the shallows of spiritual truth because we are not ready or able or willing to go deeper. The reason is that while we may be listening to God's Word we are not in fact being exercised by it nor learning from it. There is a clear rebuke in Hebrews 5:11-6:3. Too many Christians are content to stay in the beginners' class in the school of discipleship.

SEEKING GOD

Having, by their sinful disobedience, failed to glorify God the people forfeited the experience of enjoying him. But we must not think of God as being far away and remote. He did not withdraw his presence totally and we are told here of a tent of meeting, which could not be the same as the large and detailed structure of the Tabernacle because this had not yet been constructed. There was a specific tent put in place, a place for worship and for meeting with God, separate from the main camp where the people lived and worked. The fact that it was outside the camp would be a constant reminder to the people of the real measure of estrangement between them and their God. But still, those who sought the Lord would go out to the tent. It would be clear to all that some were seeking after God, and this is one of the great and necessary witnesses needed in our own day and generation. People need to see that those who claim to be Christians make it their business regularly to go to God's place of worship. No doubt some, seeing others going to seek after God, would be encouraged to go themselves and could go in company. It is good to invite people to come to church and also to bring them. Note that God made it very plain that he was not grieved with Moses, the man whom they had despised and plagued with their complaints. As soon as Moses entered the tent the visible tokens of God's glorious and gracious presence would be seen. The people would rise and worship. They would also know that this was the man who prayed for them. If God trusted Moses in this way, then they could and should trust him likewise.

33:7-11

GOD'S FRIENDS

There are still many wonderful things in these verses. No longer did Moses go up the mountain out of sight of the people; God came down to meet with Moses. What condescension there is in God. The high and lofty One who inhabits eternity and who is of purer eyes than to look on iniquity is pleased to come down to mere men and women, full of flaws and limitations (Isa. 57:15; Hab. 1:13). In the world to come, when all is fulfilled and when sin, death and Satan are all banished forever, the One who sits on the throne will dwell among his people and they shall see his face and serve him (Rev. 7:15, AV; 22:3-4). It was given to Moses to experience this at least in measure here on earth. There is a wonderful oneness of love and trust expressed in verse 11. God and Moses were trusted friends. In Numbers 12:6-8 we are told that God spoke to Moses and with

Moses in terms that were totally clear and explicit. What a privilege and what a responsibility! Of course, it meant that in many ways Moses had a very lonely and demanding life, because what he received from God he had to minister to a people who were not always eager to hear and not often grateful. Note lastly that it was when the people became aware of God's presence (and that awareness had a lot to do with Moses), that they were constrained to worship. They knew God was with Moses in a way he was not with them. Think of how in some churches you are instantly aware of the presence of God's Spirit even before the service starts, but in other places right through the service there is a sense of something lacking. Sometimes there is even an awareness of an alien spirit. When that is so, then there is something very far wrong.

33:12-16

GOD'S PRESENCE

We have been told that the Lord spoke with Moses face to face on the basis of an authentic friendship. There was an openness between them but you cannot imagine Moses ever being presumptuous or over-familiar with God. And yet we see Moses here laying his problems and fears before God in earnest and urgent intercession. He had already been assured that God would be with him personally in terms of fellowship and communion (v.11) but he wanted to know the identity of the 'angel' promised in verse 2 as the heavenly guide and enabler. Moses already had a human companion, confidant and helper in Joshua, but his concern was more for the people than for himself. After all, they were God's people, precious in his sight, and Moses pressed in upon God with what we might call a holy boldness. He did not use many words in his prayer but he was aware that, apart from God's living, active presence *with* his people and *among* them, their life and service would continue to be ineffective and liable to wander. Apart from anything else if their witness to the nations was to be effective it had to be seen beyond any shadow of doubt that they were not an ordinary people, but a people marked out for God, with evident tokens of their God's presence. They had to be a distinct people and the distinguishing mark would be the recog- nisable presence of God with them. We have in Moses' prayer an example of coming boldly to the throne of grace (Heb. 4:16). Note that his prayer was grounded in what God himself had said (v.12), and in the most reverent way Moses called upon God to make good in fact and experience what he had promised. The answer was given. The promise was made. God's presence, real and unmistakable would go with Moses and with the people. They would have the angel of his presence (Isa.

63:7-9). Moses' cry in verse 15 is simply, 'Do not send us forward on our own.' This is trust, not doubt.

THE GLORY OF GOD

We have emphasised the spiritual greatness of Moses. We have commented on his wonderful meekness, his dedication to his God-given work and his loving commitment to the people God had given into his charge. None of their neglect, criticism or contempt caused him to draw back from them. We have considered him as a man of prayer, a man of faith and a man who knew so clearly his need of God's presence if he was to be a faithful shepherd of God's people. He knew he was favoured by God and in fellowship with him (v.17) but he was not perfect. After all that God had said to him, was Moses right in asking further to see God's glory? Was this faith or was it asking for a visible token of what was unseen and eternal? We are to live by faith, not by sight (2 Cor. 5:7). The day will come when 'all His glory, full disclosed, shall open to our sight'[39] – but that day is not yet. Isaiah did not ask to see God's glory but he saw the 'train' or the skirt of the royal garments (Isa. 6:1). John, in exile, was given various glimpses of glory (Rev. 1:12-

18; 4:1-3; 21:23), but the sheer splendour of the brightness seemed to hide the Person. God did not rebuke Moses for desiring a sight of his glory but explained that all he could be allowed to see, or bear to see, was the 'afterglow' as God passed by him. In answer to the desire to see God's glory Moses was shown God's goodness and God's sovereignty (v.19). In thinking back over this experience Moses must also have been aware of the exquisite gentleness with which God dealt with him, sheltering him in the cleft of the rock. Moses must also have often pondered God's words when he said, 'There is a place by me' (near me, beside me; cf. Ps. 91:1-4). What a thought! What a privilege for sinners! This is indeed gospel truth. We are brought near by the blood of the Cross (Eph. 2:11-13). In Jesus Christ we can in fact see the glory of God (John 1:14; 2 Cor. 4:6).

34:1-4

GOD'S LAW AFFIRMED

The people of Israel would not soon forget the dramatic message of the breaking of the Law of God (Exod. 32:19), and that broken Law was there to convict and condemn them. But they had now to learn that breaking God's Law did not dispose of it, and the Law was re-written and reaffirmed by God. This time Moses had to cut the tables of stone (cf. Exod. 32:16) but the writing was by the hand of God. Regardless of the human instrument used, the Word is given by God (2 Tim. 3:16-17; 2 Pet. 1:20-21). It is God who reveals himself, and in the Law we have first a revelation of the character of God and only then a declaration of God's requirements. The people had broken faith with God and had forfeited all their rights, but God was not forsaking them. God's covenant with his people was reaffirmed in the re-writing of the Law, an indication that God's grace comes and is operative before God's Law. The title 'Freedom through Obedience' is an accurate description of the function and objective of the Ten Commandments. Human nature being what it is, if we were left to ourselves without guidance and restriction we would destroy ourselves. Moses was told to prepare himself and to present himself in the presence of God. This is the essence of worship. We do wrong when we postpone to Judgement Day the call, 'Prepare to meet your God, O Israel!' (Amos 4:12). When we deal with God there must be reality not sentiment, but at the same time we must see clearly that it is God who desires that we should come into his presence. The fact that God knows exactly who and what we are and still wants us is something that should thrill and warm our hearts. Of course there is a problem. We sin; we grieve God; we are estranged from him. What must we do? We go back to where we left the road of faith and obedience and begin again. These verses seem to be all about a new start. But a spirit of reverence is called for in verse 3. Casual and easy repentance is not the biblical pattern.

READY FOR GOD

Moses was obviously prepared to meet his God and there was no delay on God's part. He is always ready; we are the ones he has to wait for. But our time scale is not always in harmony with God's. God waited four hundred years before he moved to deliver the Israelites from Egypt and it took that time to bring the people to even a limited stage of readiness (Acts 7:6-7). Moses himself was a third of the way through his life before he began to be ready, and after that there was another 40-year spell in obscurity preparing him to be the shepherd of God's flock (Acts 7:17-34). Even at the burning bush Moses was hesitant to the point of arguing and suggesting God was making a mistake (Exod. 4:10-17). But there was no hesitation now. Moses had learned a great deal about his God through what God had said and how he had dealt with him. But now God spelled out in great detail the truth about his own person and character. God is merciful and compassionate; gracious in person, speech, attitudes and actions, slow to anger, long-suffering, remembering our frail humanity and making allowances for us in a way we tend not to do for others (Ps. 103:10-14). He is abounding, overflowing, altogether generous in his love (Eph. 3:18-19) and just as his love is steadfast or steady, so is his great faithfulness (Lam. 3:22, 23). He is a God to be counted on. He keeps or maintains steadfast love for thousands, always reaching out to them, forgiving over and over again all that is meant by iniquity, transgression and sin. What a God he is! However great our trespass, whatever we have been or done, however long we may have resisted his grace and persevered in our sins and sinning, he is willing and able to forgive. It is little wonder that on hearing God's testimony Moses pleaded with him to go with his people in spite of all their pride and perversity. This is exactly what God does.

34:5-9

THE PRICE OF SIN

Read along with these verses Psalm 130 and contrast the thoughts of God marking down in exact detail all our sins, and God forgiving. When he forgives sins he puts them away never to be recalled (Jer. 31:33-34) and he washes us clean (Isa. 1:18; 1 Cor. 6:9-11). But we must not overlook the statement that God does not clear the guilty. God does not overlook sin. He never says that sin does not matter. Its price has to be paid and its cost is infinite. All that is meant by our guilt God dealt with in his Son Jesus Christ. God laid on him the iniquity of us all (Isa. 53:6). The only way God could be righteous and still forgive, justify and accept the sinner, was by personally dealing with sin in the person of his own Son (Rom. 3:19-26). God made him sin for us, identifying Jesus with sin, making Jesus the sin-offering in order that we might be made right with God in and through him (2 Cor. 5:21). These passages help us to see something of the depth of meaning in Jesus' words from the Cross when he cried out that God had forsaken him. God does not clear the guilty, but provides for their forgiveness. But there is also a recognition that guilt is real and that the impenitent are left guilty before God. There is also the recognition that even within the forgiveness of God there are consequences that follow sin: consequences that people have to live with and repercussions that may affect their children, even on a long-term basis. Down through history we see many evidences of how wrong attitudes, actions, prejudices and injustices in one generation have affected succeeding generations. How we need to have a balanced and godly fear of sin! It was this as much as the revelation of God's grace and goodness that constrained Moses to worship and bow down before God. But his deepest and truest reaction was to ask God to come amongst his people, to forgive them, and to take them afresh as his people.

REAL COMMITMENT

God not only consented to go with his people, he outlined his plans and purposes already made for them. They had not begun to grasp, let alone see clearly, what God was going to do for them and with them. His thoughts and plans for them and their future were clear (Jer. 29:11). Read 1 Corinthians 2:9 and remember that this refers to life and service here in this world, and then ultimately to the perfection of Heaven. The outworking of God's sovereign purposes is indeed awesome. Israel was reminded that the way ahead was full of dangers and fierce oppositions from tribes already in possession of the territory promised them by God. But God would fight for them. Read the assurance given to Joshua in due time when the advance into Canaan was about to begin (Josh. 1:3-5). We are told in Judges 5:20 of a time when the very stars in their courses (whatever that may mean) fought the Israelites' battle. Later again the people were assured that the battle was the Lord's, and that he took full responsibility (2 Chr. 20:13-17). But there had to be no carelessness or overconfidence on the part of the people, nor had there to be any compromise with moral or spiritual evil (v.12). A covenant, whether it be with God or with any other person or group of persons, involves commitment and, as Jesus made so very plain, no man can serve two masters: one or the other will be despised (Matt. 6:24). Note that in verses 11-12 the danger lay in not facing up to and seeing through the inevitable warfare between truth and error. Then in verses 13-16 the spiritual danger lay in the forging of relationships with those who did not have faith in the God of salvation. Once the affections and emotions are stirred and involved, it is difficult to contract out and the heart of the believer is seduced away from its first and true love. The unequal yoke is forbidden in 2 Corinthians 6:14-7:1. The sad comment on some believers is made in Revelation 2:4. Being yoked to Jesus is life and peace (Matt. 11:28-30).

34:18-27

A YEAR OF WORSHIP

Glance back at the plain statement in verse 17. It was as if God was telling them to remember the danger and disaster in the making of the golden calf and warning them to make sure they did not go that way ever again. Visual representations of God and his truth can have a powerful and magnetic effect, and so can music, and people may be swayed by emotional reactions rather than spiritual reality. It is not surprising therefore that God now gives specific instructions regarding the pattern for worship that is both good and necessary for his people. The emphasis is not on an individual's personal devotions, although that is a vital part of the life of a believer, but on the corporate worship and the pattern of life of the gathered company of God's people. We must never regard 'going to church' as an incidental exercise, an optional extra, and there is an earnest exhortation about this given in Hebrews 10:25. If church is just 'routine' it will soon become secondary. To guard against this God gave clear instructions that cover the whole year. Some of the details of these feasts or festivals have already been given in Exodus 23:10-19. The people had to remember first of all their great redemption and deliverance from Egypt (v.18). This was God's doing and it had to be recognised that all they had by way of life flowed from that great salvation. The ritual seems to say, 'Seek first the kingdom of God and all else will fall into place' (cf. Matt. 6:33). Even at the busiest time of the farming year the Sabbath must be kept by way of testimony and obedience, not least to acknowledge and affirm faith and trust in God's promised provision (Exod. 16:22-30). The final statement in verse 20 may be understood as a promise from God in terms of Philippians 4:19. But it may also mean we are not to come before God with an empty or cold heart. Empty hands may also suggest a reluctance to give our-selves to God or to express our gratitude to God. How much we take from God and from others without a word of thanks!

DO IT GOD'S WAY

All observances, however spiritual in their nature and institution, can become mere formality when we forget that we are in fact dealing with God and being dealt with by him. The Feast of the Passover with its remembrance of the lamb slain; the Feast of Weeks, sometimes referred to as the Harvest Feast and in the New Testament as Pentecost; and the Feast of Ingathering, sometimes referred to as the Feast of Tabernacles, were the three great occasions when all the males in Israel had to gather, no doubt in some specified place. This was to remind them that although they belonged to different tribes, in different areas, with different characteristics inherited from their forefathers, they belonged essentially to one family, the family of God, called by his grace, named with his name, and summoned to his service. There may be here an emphasis to counteract both individualism and the tendency to separatism. Think of Jesus' words in John

10:16 which seem to speak of there being many kinds of sheep, various different folds, and yet one flock under one great Shepherd. This whole passage is difficult but it seems that the emphasis in verse 24 is on the future development of both people and work, together with a promise of protection by God when people were prepared to put the spiritual issues of life first. It would be easy for some unprincipled person to try to usurp another man's property and place while he was absent from home in obedience to God. Verses 25-27 echo instructions made earlier in Exodus 23:18-19. The absence of leaven or yeast means nothing tainted or sinful must be mixed into what is offered to God. The first of the first-fruits says simply that God gets the best, not the leftovers, whether of time, energy, money or enthusiasm. The end of verse 26 seems to forbid cruelty, suggesting that there is something inhuman in this practice. The truth of God and loyalty to God should never dull sensitive feelings. If this does happen, something is far wrong.

34:28

SUSTAINED BY GOD

 n interesting personal commentary on this whole experience was given by Moses much later in his life as he reviewed the way God had led his people, prior to their entering Canaan (Deut. 9:11-21, 25-29). The picture is of Moses speaking to God and God speaking to Moses. According to Deuteronomy 10:10 this was the second time he had spent 40 days and 40 nights in solitary and close company with God. To be without food that length of time and still be able to function in terms of receiving and recording God's instructions is quite amazing. Our Lord had a similar experience when tempted by the Devil, but this was to show that God's true man could resist temptation and have victory over Satan when circumstances were totally against him. There is a contrast with Adam and Eve who yielded to temptation when everything was in their favour (Matt. 4:1-11; Gen. 2:8-9; 3:1-7). The Gospel tells us that angels came and ministered to Jesus and in John 4:32 Jesus spoke of having food to eat that the disciples knew nothing of. In the Moses story we are certainly dealing with miracle, but the lesson is that when God calls to holy and demanding service he also provides and enables. How often in life's varied experiences do we find ourselves and others saying, 'I don't know how I coped!' All through his life and service Moses endured as seeing him who is invisible (Heb. 11:27). Only faith can understand that statement, and faith makes it its business to look to, and to reckon on, the things that are unseen and eternal (2 Cor. 4:18). Looking away to Jesus and fixing our eyes and hearts on him, considering him in the glory of his person and work, it will not be surprising if an inner glow of blessing begins to show on our faces without our knowing it. It is best that we should not know. We would become proud.

A SHINING FACE

When Moses came back to the people after having been in the near presence of God it was not his speech which first made a profound impression on the people. It was the radiant shining of his face that struck fear into their hearts. It is just possible, although we are not told, that on the previous occasion when Moses came down from the mountain (Exod. 32:15-16) his face had shone but immediately became clouded with righteous anger because of the flagrant sins of the people. This time, though awed by the shining of glory in Moses' face, the people responded when they were called to draw near. Then Moses, who had talked face to face with God, talked to the people and told them all the good and gracious words of instruction from God. At some point Moses must have become aware of the glory of God shining in his face because when he came to an end of what he had to tell the people he put a veil over his face so that the people would not see the glory fading. That this was the reason for the veil is made clear by Paul in 2 Corinthians 3:12-18. If the people had seen the supernatural glory fading they might well have assumed that the truth Moses had spoken was likewise temporary and non-lasting. The interesting thing is that the pattern was repeated. As Moses went back and forward into God's presence to be taught what he must teach the people the same shining and fading of the glory of his face took place. It would appear that the people of God at this stage were so immature and uncertain in their faith, trust and obedience that they needed some extraordinary sign or token to impress the truth upon them. The 'miracle' was a concession to the weakness of the people, and we must remember how resolutely Jesus refused to give signs to those who were slow to believe (Matt. 12:38-39; John 4:48).

34:29-35

REFLECTED GLORY

Read again the passage in 2 Corinthians 3:12-18, noticing especially verse 18. Paul is contrasting the passing glory of the old covenant with the permanent glory of the new covenant which was sealed with the broken body and shed blood of the Saviour. It is in Christ that we draw near to God and dwell safely and happily in his presence. Now, just as being in the presence of God transformed Moses' appearance in a way that was recognisable, so it is with us. True communion with God, far from inhibiting human personality, actually transforms it. Wesley's great hymn expresses it perfectly: 'Changed from glory into glory, till in heaven we take our place.'[40] When that time comes we are told in 1 John 3:2 that we shall be like Jesus. The interesting thing is that our Lord Jesus Christ in his human life here on earth did not have a halo or any other remarkable appearance, except at the time of his Transfiguration when the glory of perfect manhood shone out from him (Matt. 17:1-8). And yet the Bible testifies that Jesus Christ was the express image of God (Heb. 1:3) and there could be seen in him the glory of God full of grace and truth (John 1:14). When Moses went into the presence of God again and again he removed his veil and so in a very real sense his prayer, asking to see God's glory, was answered. But in applying this story, inspired by the Holy Spirit, Paul says that it is given to us to behold with unveiled face the glory of God, and in doing so we are changed, whether we are aware of it or not. As we read the Word, as we speak to God in prayer, individually or corporately, and as we gather in God's presence for worship we are beholding God. Let us turn our eyes upon Jesus and look full in his wonderful face and pray that our lives will indeed reflect something of his glory and grace so that others may see and believe.

FAITHFULNESS

These verses introduce the final section of the book. In chapters 25-31 the plans for the Tabernacle were given, the materials specified, and now the structure was to be built. If all these matters are being repeated there must be some significant spiritual lessons to be learned, and that may be seen in Exodus 39:1, 5, 7, 21, 26, 29 and 31, where the faithfulness of Moses ensured that everything was done in exact conformity to the will of God. This is of immense importance. In the work of God we are not in any sense, in any area, at any time, allowed to be 'free-lance'. We may not 'do our own thing'; we are to do all in accordance with God's revealed will which is given in Scripture. The Bible must always be the test and the guide of all standards, attitudes and practices. Whether in patterns of worship or behaviour, we must not be conformed to or squeezed into the mould and pattern of worldly thinking, because worldly thinking is man-centred, not God-centred and has to do with human satisfaction and pleasure rather than with God's pleasure and his glory (Rom. 12:1-2). The people of God are to be distinct, because unless they are, they will not shine as lights, nor function as salt in society, and they will have no real message to proclaim (2 Cor. 6:14-18; Phil. 2:14-16; Matt. 5:13-16).

If we are Christian believers we are not the same as other people, and in terms of grace and truth it needs to be seen that we have in fact been with Jesus (Acts 4:13).

RESTING

Right at the start of the vast enterprise of building the Tabernacle, which was to take much time and energy, the first emphasis is on submission to God in terms of keeping the Sabbath. In Exodus 31:16-17 the Sabbath is spoken of as a sign of the covenant between God and his people: a sign that God had committed himself to them; and to this sign the people had to respond. God wants his people for himself, for fellowship and worship, and only then for service. Jesus reflected this in his life when he called the disciples to be with him and *then* to be sent out to serve (Mark 3:13-14). It is sad to the point of tragic if we claim to be so busy in God's work that we do not have time to be with God. Our busy-ness in God's work can very easily cause us to be focussed on and driven by what *we* are doing rather than on the perfect work that God has done. The great blessing of the Sabbath is not simply rest from work, which body, mind and spirit need, but a resting in the finished work of salvation which God has accomplished in Christ. It is a recognition that all we have, all we are and all we are able to do comes from God and from God alone. Apart from him we can do nothing at all (John 15:1-5). The point of the Sabbath is for us to be with God, in fellowship with him and with his people. That, among other things, gives a sense of belonging and counteracts the debilitating loneliness that can so easily tire us out in a way that limits our service. At the beginning of the work of building the Tabernacle, and regularly right through the process, the principle and pattern of the Sabbath had to be observed. This was more important than meeting 'tight schedules'. Increasing exhaustion is not beneficial either in secular or spiritual work and if people do not stop, as God's pattern prescribes, they will grind to a halt.

35:4-19

GOD'S WORKERS

The chapter began with an emphasis on worship and communion with God. From there it moves on to generous and sacrificial giving and then to freely given service, according to the particular skills and capacities that individuals possessed. Of course, behind all this and inspiring the whole of life lies our meeting with God in worship and hearing his Word. It is the good Word of

God that kindles the desire for obedience and service. It is the awareness of all God has done for us and given to us that awakens the response of love which gives itself and its service. The terms of the 'offering' in verses 5-9 seem very rich and expensive but we must remember what Jesus said about the widow's mite and the value he gave to it (Mark 12:41-44). If we ever begin to compare our giving with that of others we have strayed spiritually. All we have is from God (1 Cor. 4:7) and all we give compares poorly with the price paid for our redemption (1 Pet. 1:18-19). Paul spoke wise and balanced words about Christian giving in 2 Corinthians 8:12-15; 9:7-12. We must note that the giving was not only in terms of money and materials, but in the practical carrying out of a great deal of very skilled work: wood-work, metal-work, filigree work in silver and gold, work with oil and lamps, and work with materials, needles and thread. There would be what is now called semi-skilled, skilled and specialist work. But there would also be the labourers carrying loads and those sweeping up and making the whole place suitable and safe for working in. Let no-one ever think that only the clever, the gifted, the university graduates, the business executives are important. People who think they are important are usually self-conscious rather than God-conscious and sometimes they actually do very little work. Read 1 Corinthians 12:22, and note especially the words 'seem' and 'indispensable'.

WILLING SERVICE

We cannot emphasise too often that in all the work of God things must be done according to what God has commanded. But this must not become the strict legalism of the Pharisees of Jesus' day, who had concocted a vast list of things not allowed, leading to a form of religion that had more to do with conforming to men's ideas than with pleasing God. There is indeed a glorious liberty given to the children of God (Rom. 8:21) and we are to stand fast in that liberty (Gal. 5:1), because Christian life is not one of bondage. There are matters of truth and behaviour about which the Bible is totally and consistently clear and no concessions can be made. But there are other issues about which each person must be persuaded in his or her own mind (Rom. 14:1-13), with the recognition that sometimes what would be permissible and harmless has to be yielded lest some younger and weaker believer should be led astray (1 Cor. 8:9-13). The vital thing in the whole business of ordering our lives to please God is our fellowship with God, our walk with him, our coming into his presence, and our glad and willing submission to the gracious instruction of his Word. We see this in verses 20-21. They listened to Moses teaching them the things of God; they went to their homes; and then they came to the work with hearts stirred and spirits moved. When that happens there is no difficulty in getting both people and provisions for the ongoing work. This is the true freewill offering to the Lord (v.29). Why is it that people can sit under the gracious ministry of God's Word and share in fellowship, professing to be blessed by both, and still show a reluctance to be available for the work of the congregation and hold back from commitment? Perhaps it is because, unlike the Israelites, they have forgotten both what they have been saved from and what they have been saved for.

35:30-36:1

TRAINING OTHERS

Two men are mentioned by name as having been called specifically by God, and filled with the Spirit in terms of skill, ability, knowledge and understanding. Their particular gifts and calling were in the realm of artistic work and in being able to teach others. The first emphasis in this is that what was being made was not simply utilitarian, made only to work effectively, but made so that it should have beauty and quality. It was for God, for God's service and for God's glory, and therefore it had to be the best. There should never be anything cheap or shoddy about our worship, whether in the music, the words we use, or the whole manner of our participation. Of course, beauty and decoration of any kind, if they become the focus of attention rather than a pointer away from themselves to God, can become a distraction and even a form of idolatry. Buildings, for example, can become more important to some people than God himself, to such an extent that if 'their church' building is closed down they do not go to church anywhere else. They fail to see that often the closure of churches is the result of spiritual unfaithfulness and a significant meanness in Christian giving over many years. The second emphasis in this passage is found in these two men teaching and training others so that the work of God never becomes dependent on the willingness or health of any individuals. Why do we try to make ourselves indispensable? Is it because we want place or power or recognition? The New Testament principle is stated in 2 Timothy 2:1-2. We must prepare for the future when others will have to take over the work, which is always God's work, not ours.

CANCEL THE OFFERING!

This must be a situation that is virtually unknown in the experience of the church in our generation. So deeply and tenderly had the hearts of the people been touched by the Word of God, the love of God, the earlier stern disciplines of God, and the restoring grace of God, that there was simply no limit to what they were willing to give for the Lord's work. The cynical would no doubt say that they were people who could well afford such sacrificial giving, but there is no suggestion in the story that this was the case. There was dedication and enthusiasm, but these were not merely emotional expressions of spiritual life and joy. The spiritual was expressed in terms of hard cash. Far from there being appeals for funds, the people had to be told to stop giving because everything had been provided for.

> It must have been both a disappointment and a frustration to those who had delayed their gifts because they could not bear to part with their treasures, and who now found that God had no further need of them. His work was finished, but they had excluded themselves from a share in it.[41]

Regrets are hard to live with. Some grow old and wish they had given themselves more truly to the service of the gospel in their earlier days. Some, because of a change of job, have moved away from their home church where they were converted and built up in their faith and then wish they had given more service and expressed more gratitude. If this makes people wiser, then it is all to the good because God is the One who restores, or makes up for, the wasted years (Joel 2:24-26, AV). Underlying the great generosity of the people was gratitude to God for all he had done for them. Think of Mary's act of costly devotion in the story of the box of precious ointment in John 12:1-8. She felt she had to express in some way her response to the Saviour's dying love. In 2 Corinthians 8:1-7 Paul spoke of the generosity of the believers in Macedonia as being an example and a challenge to others. Gratitude needs to be expressed in word and action, even if it is only a cup of water (Matt. 10:42; 25:35-45), and if we give to God but not to the person near us then God will be grieved (1 John 4:20-21).

36:8-38

THE SHOP FLOOR

This passage echoes 26:1-37 with only a few minor changes so we must try to picture the wider scene rather than studying the detail. 'As an architect delights to pore over plans or blueprints, so the pious priest would have rejoiced in this meticulous re-listing of specifications already given.'[42] If we look ahead to Exodus 40:1 we will see that the present passages are still dealing with the gathering together of all the prepared curtains, posts and hooks. Many a time the scene must have looked and felt quite chaotic. Moses and the people must at times have felt dismayed because it seemed no real progress was being made. No doubt Moses, the pastor as well as the teacher and leader of the people, would have reassured them that their labour was not in vain in the Lord (1 Cor. 15:58). In and through all the bustle of work and seeming chaos, Moses knew that God was with them and that they were working together under his direction (1 Cor. 3:9; 2 Cor. 6:1). He endured and he coped because he was sure of this (Heb. 11:27). Of course there are times when the work has to go on without the encouragement of plentiful supplies and eager workers. Jeremiah's ministry was like that. Things in the nation then were going down, but God was in it, and the prophet, though at times he staggered, endured to the end. Visible signs of progress and evidences of success always appeal but we need to remember, trite though it may be to say it, that God looks for faithfulness not success (1 Cor. 4:2-5). If we remember that the church on earth is a factory as well as a display-window we will understand why things often look chaotic. It certainly should not be a museum!

GOD'S MERCY SEAT

This is the outworking of 25:10-40 and 30:1-10. In the earlier instructions about the Tabernacle, the account started with the heart of all the worship, namely the Ark of the Covenant and everything worked outward from there. Now that the actual structure was about to be erected, it is logical that they should start with the outer framework and curtains and then, when the inner tent was erected inside the courtyard, the furniture would be put in place. Perhaps we should see in the repetition of all the immense detail a testimony to the exactness of Moses' obedience and that of the workers. Again we emphasise the familiar words, 'God's work must be done in God's way.' A great deal of confusion, and at times harm, is caused to the long-term work of the gospel by the intrusion of people's 'bright ideas' which often have a degree of entertainment in them and which usually prove to be short-lived. The reference to the cherubim (vv.7-9) overshadowing the Mercy Seat should remind us of the hymn that calls, 'Approach, my soul, the mercy seat, where Jesus answers prayer; There humbly fall before His feet, for none can perish there.'[43] Think of Genesis 3:22-24 where the cherubim were set at the gate of the Garden to prevent sinner man from coming back into the presence of God. But now, the cherubim seem to be pointing to God's redeeming love. The blood-sprinkled Mercy Seat speaks of pardon, reconciliation, acceptance and free access into the very presence of God. It speaks of the Cross where the Saviour, the Lamb of God, died to take away sin. We should be grateful for the inspired words of hymn-writers who express so well the truths of the gospel. Think of Horatius Bonar's words about the Cross:

> Here is pardon's pledge and token,
> Guilt's strong chain for ever broken,
> Righteous peace securely made.[44]

Think long and well and with thanksgiving about God's mercy seat.

38:1-31

GOD'S CHURCH

After the actual Tabernacle was prepared the next priority was the furniture of the courtyard. In verse 1 there is mention of the altar of burnt offering because without the appropriate sacrifice for sin no-one can come to God. In verse 8 there is mention of the basin for ceremonial washing, because those who would come into the presence of God must be clean. The basin was made from the bronze of the mirrors given by the women, and these mirrors were possibly their most precious possessions and had to do with their own adornment and appearance. It is not clear in what way these women ministered at the door of the tent of meeting. They may have been 'cleaning women' or perhaps doorkeepers, such as are spoken of in Psalm 84:10. Some suggest that the prophetess Anna referred to in Luke 2:36-38 may have been one of the New Testament equivalents of the women spoken of here. In verses 24-31 we are told of the total of men numbered in Israel (v.26), and if we added the younger men, the women and children, we have indeed a vast concourse of people and that helps us to see that the huge amounts of money involved need not be any exaggeration. A congregation of this size makes us gasp and helps us to understand something of the burden Moses carried and why he was so insistent that without God's presence he did not want to go forward (Exod. 33:12-16). Such vast numbers could make those now working in small fellowships feel rather insignificant but that is not necessary. Always remember that, whatever our numerical strength, when we gather for worship and when we serve in the gospel, we are in living and vital fellowship with all those in every place who call on the name of the Lord (1 Cor. 1:2). God's church is one great company of the redeemed and it numbers ten thousand times ten thousand, and thousands of thousands (Rev. 5:11). That will become evident one day and we will then realise what we have been involved in.

REDEEMING LOVE

We pause briefly from the immense and bewildering detail of these chapters. Read Hebrews 12:1-3, 12-13, 18-24, 28-29. What we are involved in is greater by far than the situations we have been reading about in Exodus. All the detail of the Tabernacle, its sacrifices and worship, and the significant place and function of the High Priest, point forward to the spiritual realities accomplished in Jesus Christ. His sacrifice was the atoning death of the true Lamb of God. His was the precious blood that was shed to make peace with God (Col. 1:19-20). If we have wearied of the details we have been reading, and if we have begun to feel that the way into God's presence seems to be immensely and impossibly difficult, full of barriers, restrictions, and requiring so much by way of costly sacrifice, then we need to be reminded that sinners have no automatic right to come into the presence of God, the God who is of purer eyes than to look on sin (Hab. 1:13). Because we are sinners by nature, choice and practice, we have forfeited all right to come to God and to dwell with him. We stand guilty before God and can say or do nothing on our own behalf (Rom. 3:9-10,19-20). We are separated from God, excluded from him on every level (Eph. 2:12-13). In every sense we are helpless and hopeless. But the symbolism of the Tabernacle points to the gospel which tells sinners that Jesus saves. There is a way back to God. There is a God who calls us back, a God who wants us, a God who himself, in the Person of his own dear Son, paid the price of sin. The whole Bible declares the redeeming love of God, the God who spared not even his own Son but gave him up for us all (Rom. 5:6-11; 8:32).

39:1-31

THE HOLINESS OF GOD

Read Isaiah 6:1-5; Daniel 10:4-9; Revelation 1:12-18. These and many other passages speak of the holiness of God (v.30), a theme sadly lacking in much evangelical preaching. As a result there is often lacking conviction of sin, the call to repentance, and a genuine awareness of the need for salvation. In much contemporary Christian praise there is a jolly, almost careless spirit, and we need to recover the truths and emphases of such hymns as this:

Eternal Light! eternal Light!
How pure the soul must be,
When, placed within Thy searching sight,
It shrinks not, but, with calm delight,
Can live, and look on Thee!

The spirits that surround Thy throne
May bear the burning bliss;
But that is surely theirs alone,
Since they have never, never known
A fallen world like this.

O how shall I, whose native sphere
Is dark, whose mind is dim,
Before the Ineffable appear,
And on my naked spirit bear
The uncreated beam?

There is a way for man to rise
To that sublime abode:
An offering and a sacrifice,
A Holy Spirit's energies,
An advocate with God.

These, these prepare us for the sight
Of holiness above:
The sons of ignorance and night
May dwell in the eternal Light,
Through the eternal Love![45]

A WORTHY DWELLING PLACE

These verses record the finishing of all the work. The whole structure and its worship would have been ineffective without the God-ordained High Priest who represented the people and carried them on his shoulders and heart into the presence of God. The details have been commented on in the notes on chapter 28. Everything points forward to Jesus, our great High Priest, spoken of in so many passages in the Epistle to the Hebrews. Again we note the immense detail and what that must have demanded in terms of concentration and careful supervision. We tend to think something less demanding would have been sufficient. But it was all for God, and that means it had to be worthy and well done. There is a tendency to think that work for the church does not call for the same quality, value and effort as for our homes and businesses. The prophet Haggai had some searching observations to make on that theme (Hag. 1:1-11). All the prepared material was brought to Moses (v.33) who seems to have (with help, no doubt) reviewed all the preparation. It represented an immense amount of work and of staying power on the part of the people, and it was all preparation. The Tabernacle had not yet been erected. In a sense they had nothing to show yet for all this God-directed work. But one thing was clear to Moses. There had been the diligent obedience of faith. The work had been carried out as God had commanded and as a result the people were blessed (v.43). We have spoken again and again of the need for God's work to be done in God's way, and we see now that such work will not lack God's blessing. It may be, of course, that some will not recognise God's blessing because they are looking for something that can be measured in merely human terms. God's way is perfect (Ps. 18:30), and the believer who is pure or single in heart will see God (Matt. 5:8) and be aware of his presence and working.

40:1-15

GOD'S TIMING

The work of preparation was now complete and all the parts for the Tabernacle had been made ready. But Moses did not go right ahead with the erection of this significant place of worship. He waited upon God until he received direct and specific instruction to start the building (v.2). This is what Moses had done all along from the time when God first began to give instructions for the Tabernacle (Exod. 24:12-18). He had learned from God's dealings with him and from his own earlier blunders because of hasty decisions (Exod. 2:11-15).

God has his clear times and seasons, and keeps to them, revealing his will and his ways at the right time (Heb. 1:1-2; Acts 1:7). Think of this in terms of our Lord's life on earth. He knew the purpose for which he had come into the world and he rested in the 'time-table' of his Father. At various points the enemies would have 'sprung the trap' but they were prevented because Jesus' time had not yet come (John 7:30; 8:20). Then the time came when Jesus said, 'Father, the time has come' (John 17:1). We should never want to take the reins into our own hands because our knowledge is so limited. We must learn to wait upon God, not least because those who do so renew their strength and release their capacities (Isa. 40:28-31). In waiting, we must also learn to rest in the Lord (Ps. 37:7, AV). To wait with fretting impatience is not only negative, it is a denial of faith. God always knows what he is doing and when is the right time for doing it. When we wait on God, and it seems that delay continues, we should not doubt and allow ourselves to become despondent. Rather we should speak to God, maintain our fellowship with him, learn the lessons he wants to teach us, and allow his gracious Spirit to kindle both hope and expectation. It was when the time had fully come, and not until then, that God sent forth his Son (Gal. 4:4).

THE TENT OF MEETING

This would be a good reading for New Year's Day. It is difficult to calculate dates exactly but Bishop Ellicott in his commentary argues that the Israelites had left Egypt on the fourteenth day of the first month (Exod. 12:2, 6), reaching the wilderness of Sinai in the course of the third month, Sivan. They then camped in front of Mount Sinai (Exod. 14:1, 2). The two long absences of Moses in the Mount occupied nearly three months, and were separated by an interval probably of several days. It must have been the sixth or seventh month before the work was begun, and very late in the year, the eleventh or twelfth month, before it was finished. That means the new year was now approaching, and its first day was the most natural choice for the inauguration of the new structure. The choice of the day was, of course, made by God, not by Moses or by the people or by a committee! Note carefully the description 'The Tent of Meeting' (v.2). This is the purpose of the whole detailed scheme: that God should come and dwell in the midst of his people. Right through the passage there is the repetition of the words 'you shall' (AV). In the NIV it is a series of instructions: place, bring, anoint, take. Do you see how eager God is to make sure his people do not go wrong? If God is going to come to dwell with us, is it not right that we should prepare the way of the Lord? Read Isaiah 40:1-5, 9; Malachi 3:1-4. We have to be serious and realistic if we are to deal with God and if he is to dwell with us.

EVERYTHING IN ITS PLACE

Under the direction of Moses the people erected the Tabernacle and placed everything in its God-appointed place. We have already studied the spiritual significance of all the details mentioned here but two things need to be noted and emphasised. Right through the passage there is a repetition of the words, 'as the Lord commanded'. Faith and obedience, worship and obedience, spirituality and obedience go together and must never be separated. Jesus made this perfectly clear when he said, 'If you love me you will obey what I command' (John 14:15). The second thing to note is that at the heart of the whole system of worship in Israel there stood the ark of the testimony and the mercy seat (Exod. 40:3, 20-21). What God had spoken, his covenant of grace and his Word of Law are and must always be the supreme rule of faith and life. The Shorter Catechism expresses it well in the words: 'The Scriptures principally teach what man is to believe concerning God, and what duty God requires of man.' The tragedy in our day is that the general public is almost totally ignorant of the Bible and, sad to say, even many Christians know only snatches of Scripture and have very little grasp of the sweep, the unity and integrity of the Word of God. Both Moses and the people were aware that they were working under the direction of God and they had the promise of God that he would meet with them and dwell among them (Exod. 25:22). But as they worked, no doubt getting tired in the process, had they any real idea of what the presence of God would mean? Have people any idea what it really means when at Christmas time we speak about 'God with us'? It means that God is with us in a way that does not fill us with fear. Psalm 90:1-2, 13-17 may well have been prayed by Moses at this time.

40:34-38

THE GLORY OF THE LORD

These verses record the climax of all the preparations we have studied and indicate a people ready for the next stage of God's plan and programme of salvation. The glory of the Lord filled the tabernacle. In the introduction to the Christmas story we are told of the glory of God shining over the shepherds. That glory may not now be visible but the reality is still there. There was no shining glory over the stable at Bethlehem and there was a cloud of darkness at the Cross. But God was there! If we really believed that God is with us, in spite of all our flaws and failures, and if we really believed the promise of the Saviour that he would be with us at all times and in all places, all through time (Matt. 28:20), what a difference it would make to our peace, assurance, enjoyment and effectiveness in the service of the gospel. Think of what it must have meant to the Israelites when *the* cloud covered the tent of meeting. This was not any cloud. It was the same cloud that had accompanied, directed and protected them earlier in their journeys (Exod. 13:20-22; l4:19-20). What a reminder this was that the God who had begun the work of their salvation and deliverance was still with them to bring forward that work to its completion (Phil. 1:6). Think how the story of Exodus started with a depressed, demoralised and disillusioned people who were slaves in Egypt; now they were free and on their way to a destiny of service and fulfilment. If the erecting of the Tabernacle was done in one day it must have been at least dusk when it was completed and we must imagine the feeling of the people as the brilliant appearance of the glory of God came down, entered and filled the entire dwelling. We, who live in the gospel age, can now think of the same cloud which signifies the presence and the glory of God in the story of the Transfiguration of Jesus in Matthew

17:1-5 and in the account of the Ascension in Acts 1:7-9. But we must remember that God's presence is not always indicated by visible signs. He often hides himself so that we learn to live by faith (Hab. 3:4, AV; John 20:29).

40:34-38

GOD WITH US

The glory of the Lord filled the Tabernacle. That clear statement made it plain to the people that this was no mere human structure. God was there. From all the detail we have studied it is clear that the Tabernacle was a wonderful place of worship, a thing of beauty inside, as the temple was in Solomon's day, and later in Jesus' day. But apart from the glory of God's presence buildings, however grand, are really nothing but examples of the brilliance of human achievement. It follows that no matter how simple and devalued a building may be in the eyes of men, if God is there then it is a significant building in a full spiritual sense. It has been emphasised again and again that all the building of the Tabernacle, down to the smallest detail, was done in obedience to God's command: the obedience of faith. But when the obedience of faith is absent; when God's people grow casual, complacent and careless in the way they live and serve, the presence of the glory of God may not simply be clouded, it may depart. Recall the solemn story in 1 Samuel 2:12, 17; 3:1; 4:21-22 when those who served the Lord had backslidden and were presumptuous in their sinning. The glory departed! Note also that in those days even in the House of God the Word of God was scarce. The absence of the Word and the absence of the glory were connected. Read the story of the dedication of the Temple in the time of Solomon in 1 Kings 8:1-11, 27-30. At the heart of the House of God there was the Word of God and the glory of God came down to confirm and seal that Word.

40:34-38

GOD'S TRUSTED MAN

Right at the end of the story we are once again caused to think of the man Moses. We know that no-one is indispensable in God's work and it is when people begin to think they are, or when they begin to think they are more important than others, that their usefulness in service begins to diminish and even come to an end. We should never forget Paul's determination to keep 'self' under control lest he be disqualified from further service (1 Cor. 9:24-27). That Moses was a strong character is obvious but it is not always recognised that part of his strength came from his meekness (Num. 12:1-3) and part from his close walk with God (Exod. 33:11). In Acts 7:17-44 we are given a panoramic view of the history and significance of Moses. He was a man of capacity, with a magnificent education in Egypt, but that does not necessarily make a man useful in God's service. In his early days his enthusiasm and sense of justice were precipitate, lacking in control, and he was removed from the public eye. For 40 years he proved himself in secular affairs, learning the demand and discipline of being a shepherd. Even then, as Exodus 3:10-11; 4:1,10-14 make plain, he was hesitant about God's call, giving more attention to his own perceived feelings of incapacity than to God's clear call. He had to learn that God does not make mistakes about his choices, his timing or his directions. It was as Moses learned what God is like, and as he learned to know God in terms of worship, fellowship, service and obedience, that he became a great man of faith. The summary of Moses' faith and life in Hebrews 11:23-29 is brief but vivid. He endured as seeing him who is invisible. He was aware of God. He was persuaded that he was under orders from God, the God who had covenanted to be with him. In these verses in Hebrews we must not forget the vital part played by the faith of Moses' parents, nor the clear choice that Moses made. He chose to go with and to suffer with the people of God rather than to have the promotion, the profit and the pleasures of sin in a worldly life. What an example for all of us!

40:34-38

THE FUTURE

As we come to the end of our long series of studies in Exodus we must note that the last verse speaks of journeys, making it plain that the end is not yet. The children of Israel were pointed ahead to the future, and so are we. We are on the way with God and all God's dealings with us in instruction and discipline are to prepare and equip us for the service that lies ahead of us in this world and the next. Never forget that in Heaven we shall serve him who is the God of our salvation and we shall see his face (Rev. 22:3-4). We do not go into the future alone but neither do we presume upon God's presence. He is not unwilling but we must ask him to help us learn the lessons he taught the Israelites of old. We may not have visible pillars of cloud and fire but we have the sure Word of God (2 Pet. 1:19) that equips us (2 Tim. 3:16-17), that shines on our path (Ps. 119:105), that feeds and builds us up (1 Pet. 1:22-2:3) and that has a washing and cleansing effect on mind, heart, spirit and life (Eph. 5:26). Of course it is possible to close our eyes to God's light, and we will do so if we are doing wrong in our lives (John 3:19-20). We will be insensitive to all the indications of encouragement God is giving us if we are so preoccupied with ourselves and what we are doing that we forget God. We can in fact turn our backs upon the pillar of cloud and fire. We need to fix our hearts (Ps. 57:7, AV) and our minds on God (Isa. 26:3-4). The life of faith takes effort. We have to lay hold on eternal life (1 Tim. 6:12). We do well to pray:

> Guide me, O Thou great Jehovah,
> Pilgrim through this barren land;
> I am weak, but Thou art mighty;
> Hold me with Thy powerful hand:
> Bread of heaven,
> Feed me till my want is o'er.
>
> ...
> Let the fire and cloudy pillar
> Lead me all my journey through:
> Strong Deliverer,
> Be Thou still my strength and shield.[46]

NOTES

1 A. Cole, *Exodus*, Tyndale Old Testament Commentaries (IVP, Leicester, 1973).

2 F. L. Hosmer, 'Thy Kingdom come', *The Church Hymnary, Revised Edition (RCH)*, no. 153.

3 F. W. Faber, 'Workman of God!', *RCH*, no. 520.

4 Idem.

5 T. Olivers, 'The God of Abraham praise', *RCH*, no. 571.

6 A. Cole, ibid., p. 68.

7 Ibid., pp. 77-8 (quoting Driver).

8 W. Cowper, 'God moves in a mysterious way', *RCH*, no. 31.

9 I. Watts, 'When I survey the wondrous cross', *RCH*, no. 106.

10 W. Williams, 'Guide me, O Thou great Jehovah', *RCH*, no. 564.

11 A. M. Toplady, 'A Sovereign Protector I have', *RCH*, no. 560.

12 J. Montgomery, 'Stand up and bless the Lord', *RCH*, no. 233.

13 T. Kelly, 'We sing the praise of Him who died', *RCH*, no. 109.

14 R. Heber, 'Holy, holy, holy, Lord God Almighty', *RCH*, no. 1.

15 T. Binney, 'Eternal Light!', *RCH*, no. 36.

16 W. Shakespeare, *Othello*, III.iii, lines 157-61.

17 F. W. Faber, 'My God, how wonderful Thou art', *RCH*, no. 27.

18 A. Cole, ibid., p. 165.

19 *The Illustrated Bible Dictionary* (IVP, Leicester, 1980), vol. 2, pp. 931-5.

20 J. Morison, ''Twas on that night when doomed to know', *RCH*, no. 312.

21 F. W. Faber, ibid.

22 H. Bonar, 'Here, O my Lord, I see Thee face to face', *RCH*, no. 323.

23 W. C. Smith, 'Immortal, invisible', *RCH*, no. 12.

24 H. Bonar, ibid.

25 P. Bliss, 'Man of Sorrows!', *RCH*, no. 693.

26 F. Hogan, *Words of Life from Exodus* (Collins Fount Paperbacks, London, 1984), p. 198.

27 F. Hogan, ibid., p. 200.

28 Scottish Paraphrases, no. 48, v. 1.

29 Scottish Paraphrases, no. 22, v. 3.

30   Scottish metrical Psalms, no. 43, v. 3.

31   Scottish metrical Psalms, no. 89, v. 15.

32   C. J. Ellicott, ed., *A Bible Commentary for English Readers* (Cassell & Co., Ltd., London, n.d.), vol. 1, p. 301.

33   Scottish Paraphrases, no. 58, v. 2.

34   A. M. Toplady, 'Rock of Ages', *RCH*, no. 413.

35   G. Matheson, 'Make me a captive, Lord', *RCH*, no. 464.

36   A. Cole, ibid., p. 217.

37   W. Temple, *Readings in St. John's Gospel* (Macmillan and Co. Ltd., London, 1950), p. 68.

38   F. R. Havergal, 'Who is on the Lord's side?', *RCH*, no. 519.

39   Scottish Paraphrases, no. 63, v. 4.

40   C. Wesley, 'Love Divine', *RCH*, no. 479.

41   A. Cole, ibid., p. 235.

42   A. Cole, idem.

43   J. Newton, 'Approach, my soul, the mercy-seat', *RCH*, no. 451.

44   H. Bonar, 'By the Cross of Jesus standing', *RCH*, no. 104.

45   T. Binney, 'Eternal Light', *RCH*, no. 36.

46   W. Williams, ibid.